THE HOW TO DRAW BOOK FOR KIDS

Adventure!

A SIMPLE STEP-BY-STEP GUIDE TO DRAWING 100 FUN AND EXCITING THINGS

WRITTEN AND ILLUSTRATED BY
Jacy Corral

This book belongs to:

Want free goodies?!

Email us at

modernkidpress@gmail.com

Title the email "How to Draw for Kids Adventure!" and we'll send some goodies your way!

Follow us on Instagram! @modernkidpress

Questions & Customer Service:
Email us at modernkidpress@gmail.com!

The How to Draw Book for Kids: Adventure! A Simple Step-by-Step Guide to Drawing Fun and Exciting Things
©Modern Kid Press & Jacy Corral. All rights reserved. No part of this publication may be reproduced, distributed, or transmitted, in any form or by any means, including photocopying, recording, or other electronic or mechanical methods, without prior written permission of the publisher, except in the case of brief quotations embodied in critical reviews and certain other noncommercial uses permitted by copyright law.

Back cover photo: Amanda Arneill.

Printed in China

TABLE OF CONTENTS

Camping.............................1

Pirates..............................37

Sports..............................73

Medieval Times..............107

Things that Go................145

How To Use this Book

1. Draw the black lines from the first drawing.

2. Add the black lines from each additional step.

3. If you get stuck, practice by tracing the final image. Then, try drawing it yourself from the start!

You can do it!

Campfire

1

2

3

4

5

6

Camping

Campfire

7

8

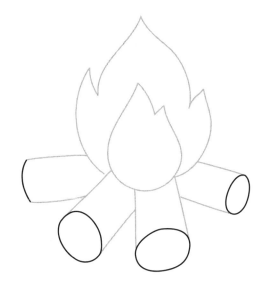

9

10

Camping | 3

Compass

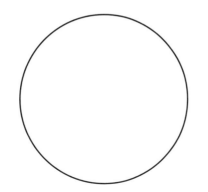
1

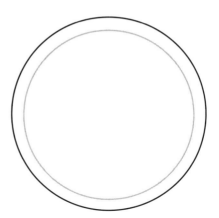
2

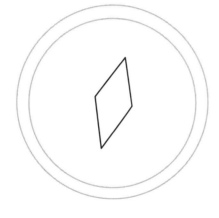
3

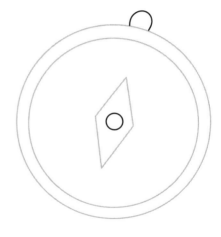
4

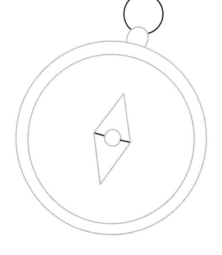
5

6

Camping

Marshmallow on a Stick

1

2

3

4
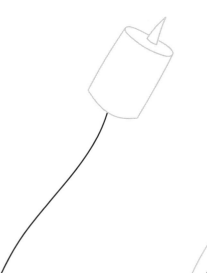

5

6
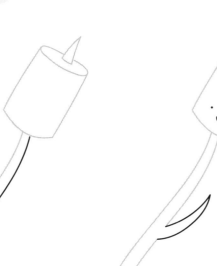

Camping | 5

 # Tent

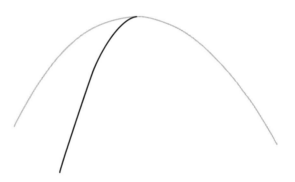

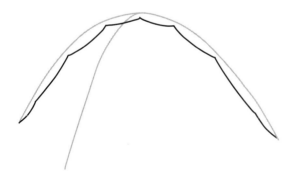

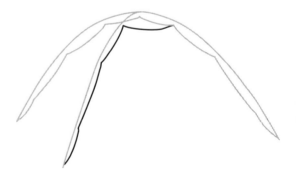

Tent

5

6

7

8

# Trail Map

1

2

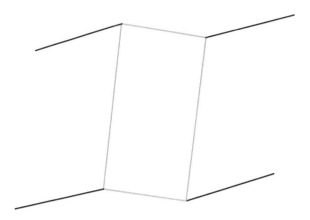

3

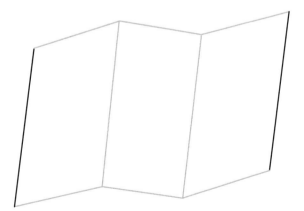

4

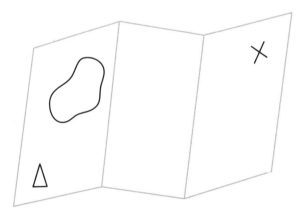

Trail Map

5
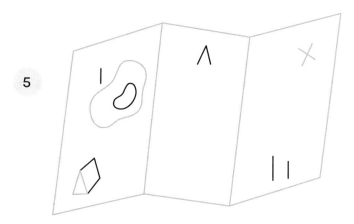

6
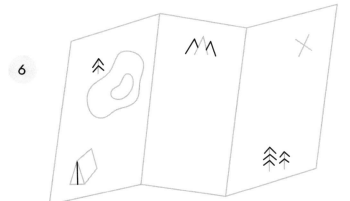

7
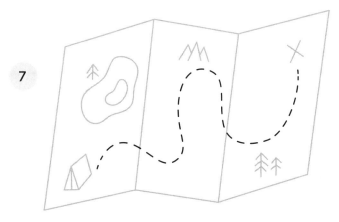

Flashlight

10 | Camping

Flashlight

9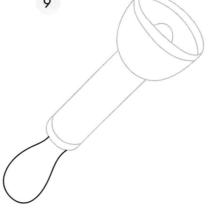

10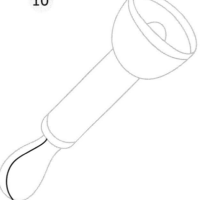

11

12

13

14

Multitool Knife

1
2
3
4
5
6
7
8

Camping

Multitool Knife

9
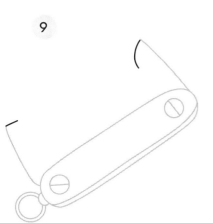

10
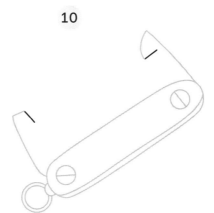

11
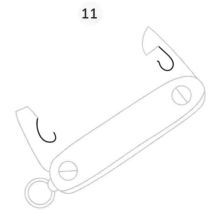

12
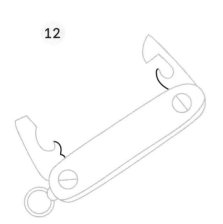

13
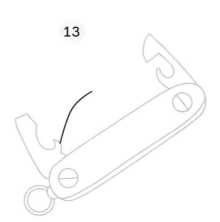

14
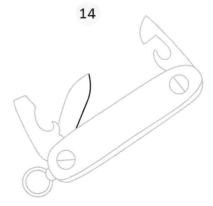

15
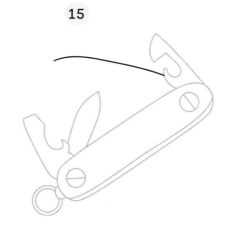

16
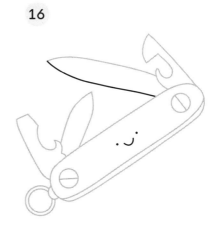

Camping | 13

Rope

1.
2.
3.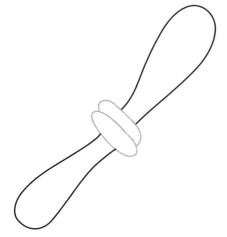
4.
5.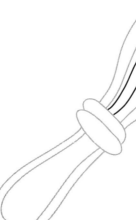
6.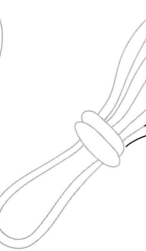

14 | Camping

Rope

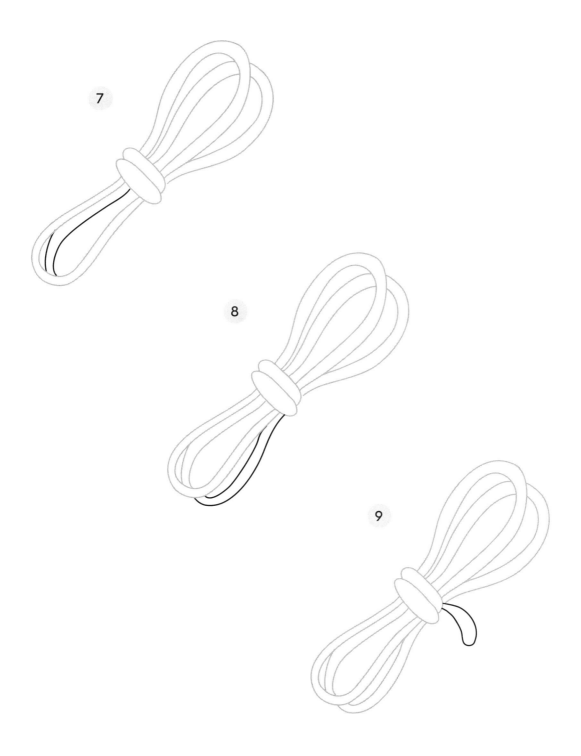

Camera

1

2

3

4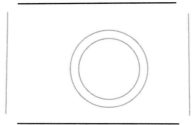

5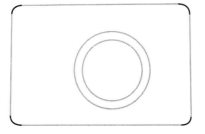

6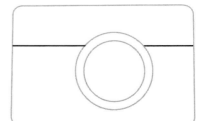

16 | Camping

Camera

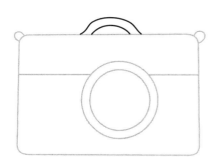
7

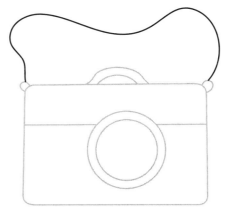
9

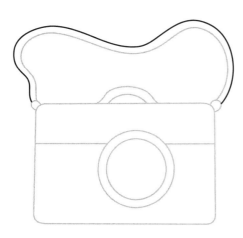
8

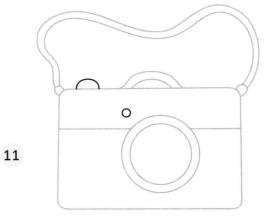
11

12

Camping | 17

Hiking Boot

1

2

3

4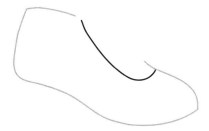

5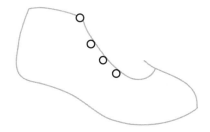

6

7

Hiking Boot

8

9

10

11

12

13

14

15

Camping | 19

Backpack

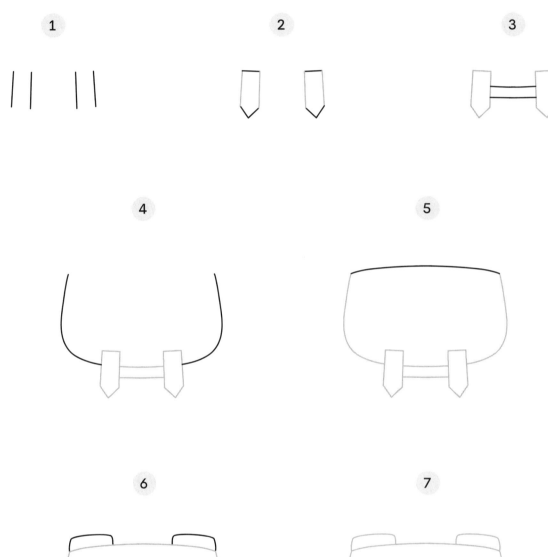

Camping

Backpack

8
9
10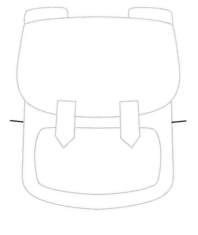
11
12
13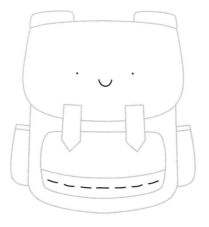

Camping | 21

Lantern

1

2

3

4

5

6

7

8

9

Lantern

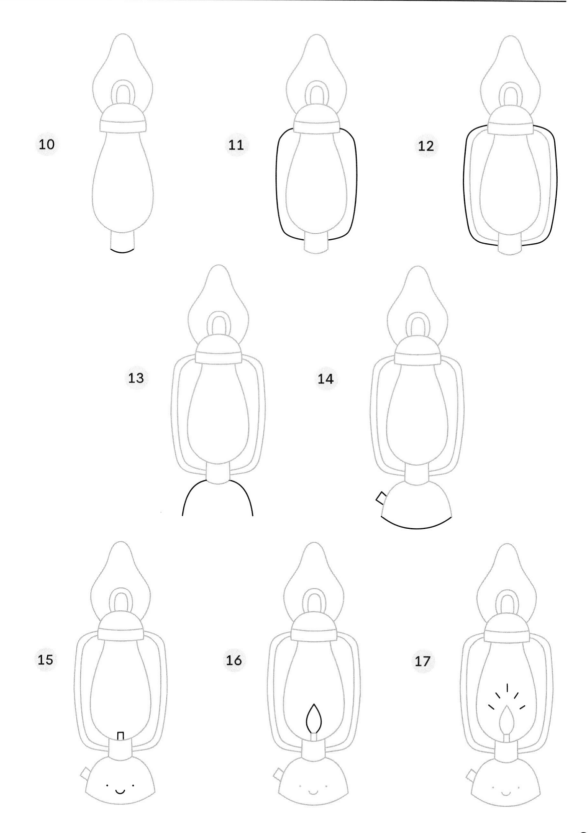

Camping | 23

Oars

1

2

3

4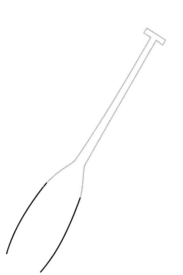

5

6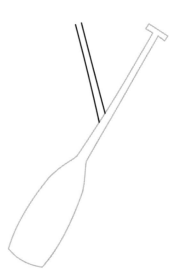

24 | Camping

Oars

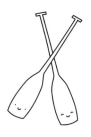

7

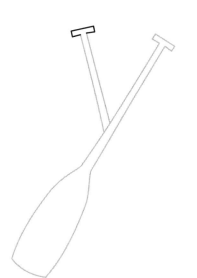

8

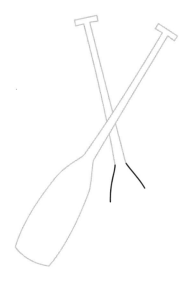

9

10

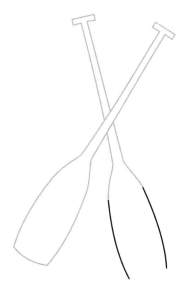

11

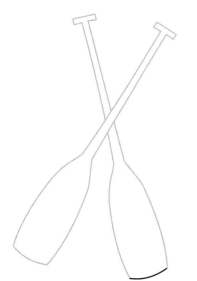

12

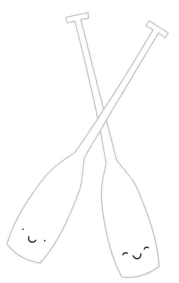

Camping | 25

Sleeping Bag

1

2

3
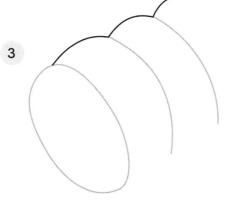

4
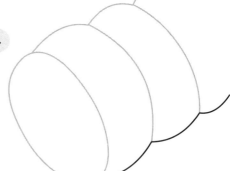

5
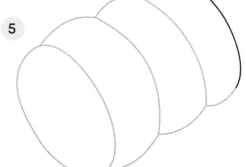

Sleeping Bag

6
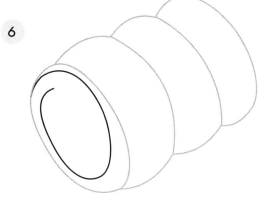

7
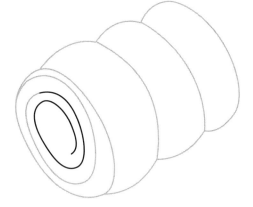

8
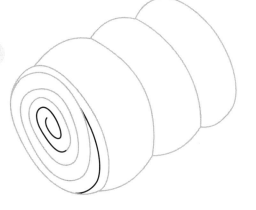

9

10

Camping | 27

Pinecone

1
2
3

4
5
6

 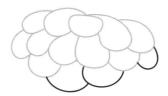 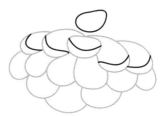

7
8

 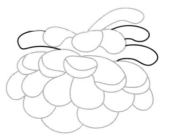

Pinecone

9

10

11

12

13

14

15

Camping | 29

Binoculars

1

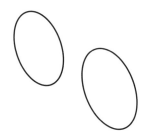

2

3

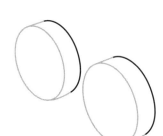

4

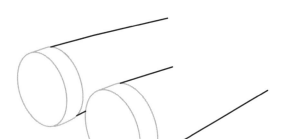

5

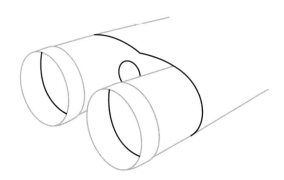

Binoculars

6
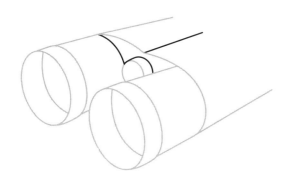

7
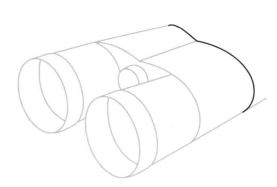

8
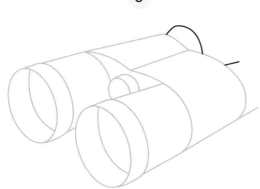

9
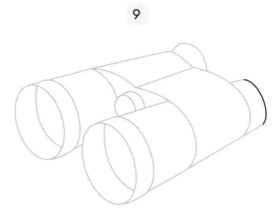

10
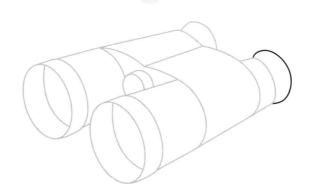

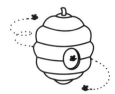

Beehive

1

2

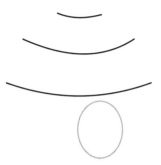

3

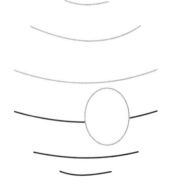

4

5

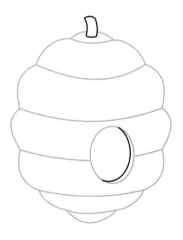

6

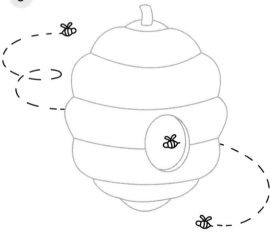

32 | Camping

Hatchet

1

2

3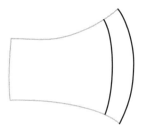

4

5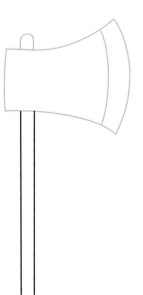

6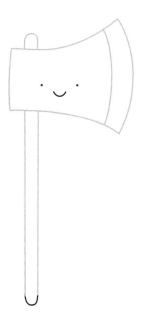

Camping | 33

Whistle

1

2

3

4

5

6

7

8

Camping

Whistle

9

10

11
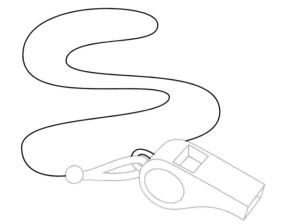

12
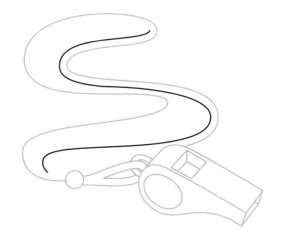

13

Camping | 35

Leaves

Treasure Chest

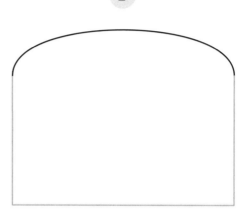

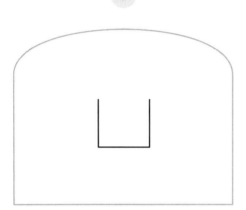

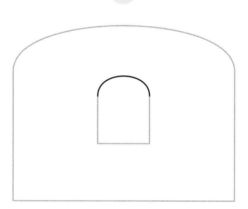

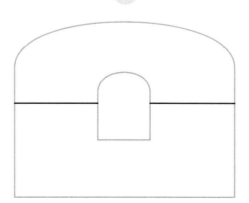

Treasure Chest

6

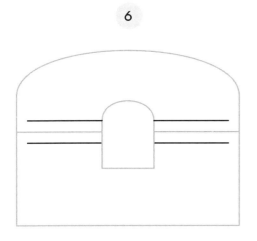

7

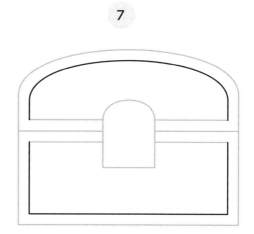

8

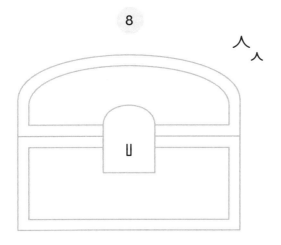

9

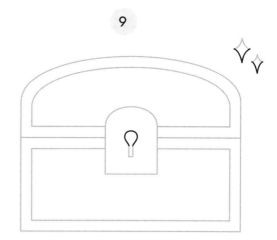

10

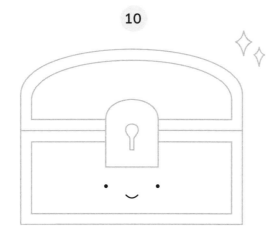

Pirates | 39

Pirate's Hook

1

2

3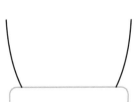

4

40 | Pirates

Pirate's Hook

5

6

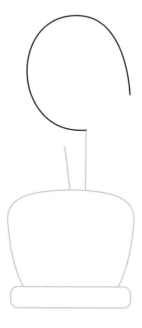

7

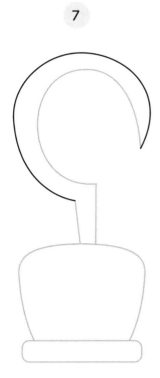

8

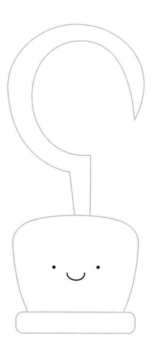

Skull and Crossbones

1
2
3
4
5
6
7
8
9

42 | Pirates

Skull and Crossbones

10

11

12

13

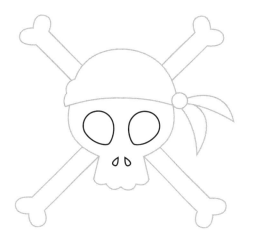

Pirate Sword

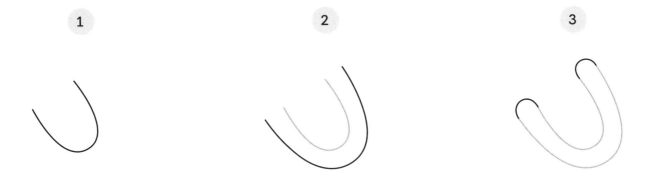

Pirate Sword

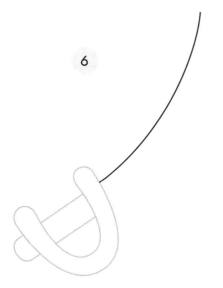

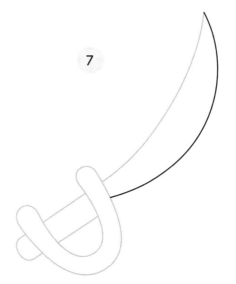

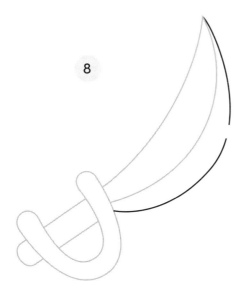

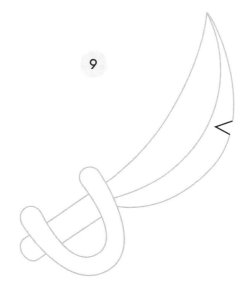

Pirates | 45

Barrel

1

2

3

4

Barrel

5

6
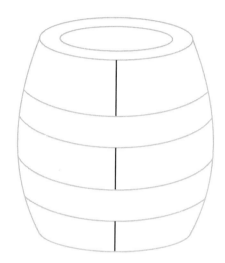

7
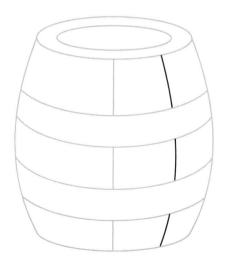

8
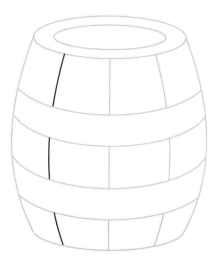

Pirate Flag

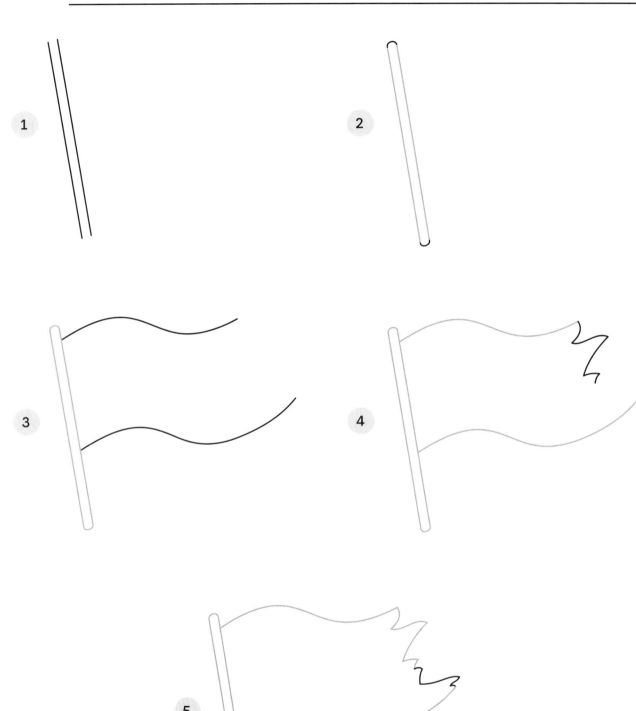

Pirate Flag

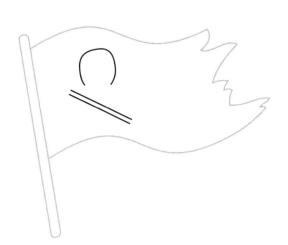

Pirates | 49

Poison

1

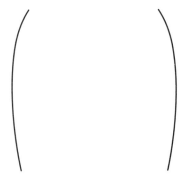

2

3

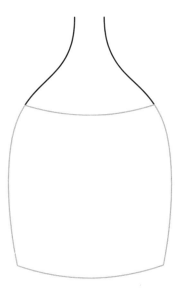

4

Poison

5
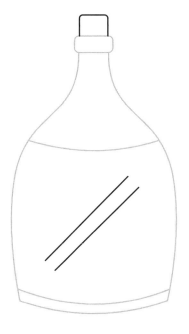

6
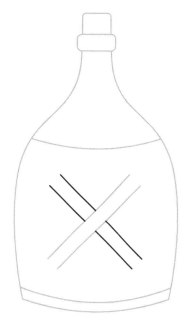

7
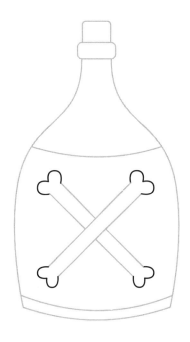

8
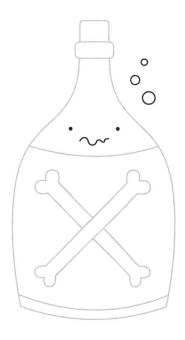

Pirates | 51

# Pirate Ship

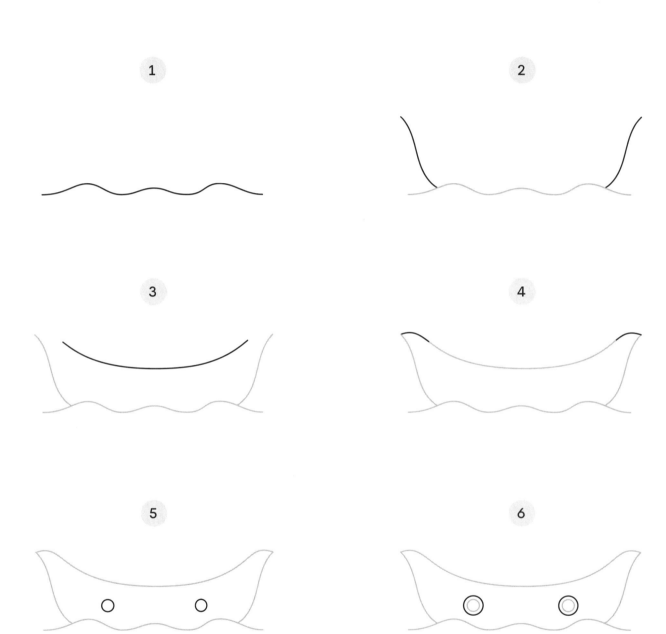

Pirate Ship

7

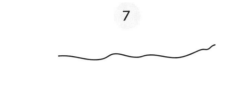

8

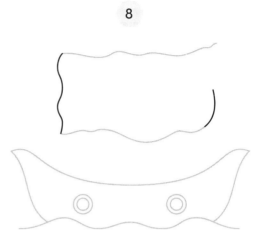

9

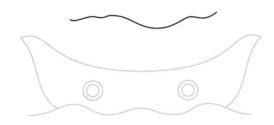

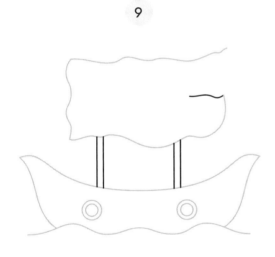

10

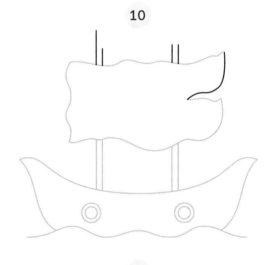

11

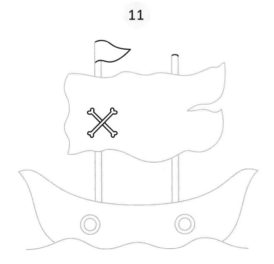

12

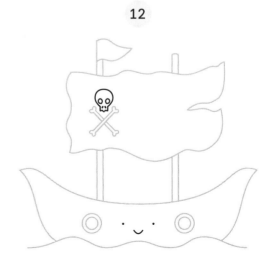

Pirates | 53

Treasure Map

Treasure Map

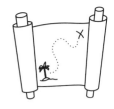

4

5

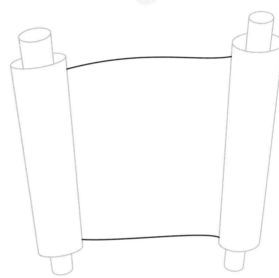

6

Pirates | 55

Message in a Bottle

1
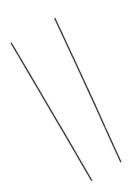

2
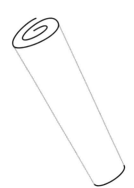

3

4
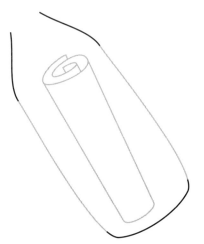

Message in a Bottle

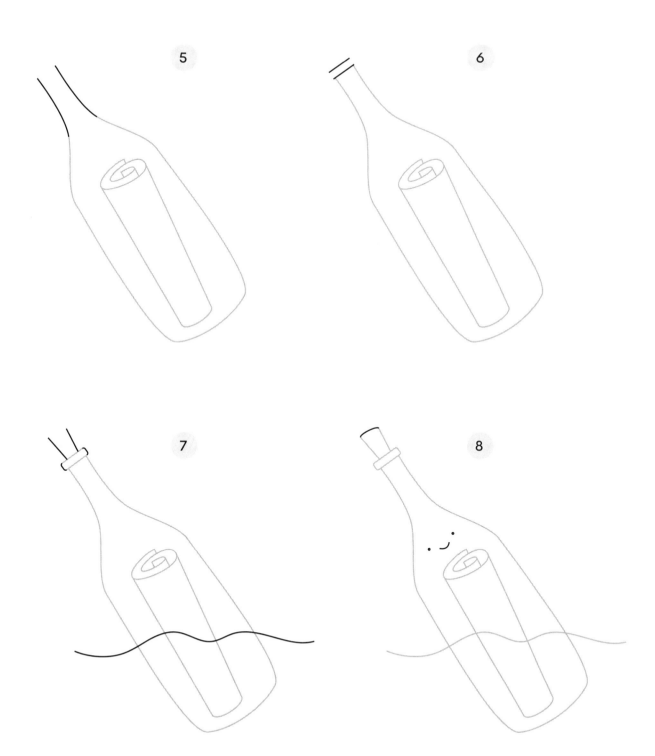

Pirates | 57

Telescope

1

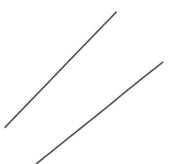

2

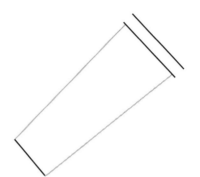

3

4

Telescope

5

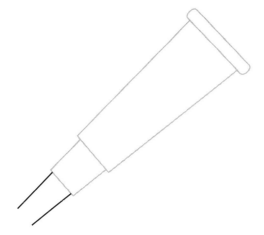

6

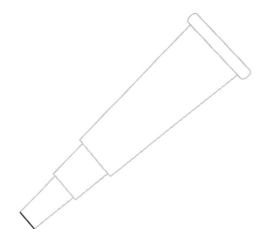

7

8

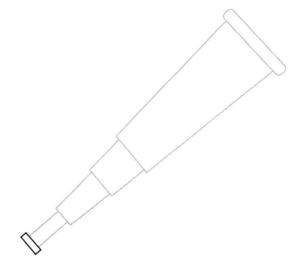

Pirates | 59

Cannon

1

2

3

4

5

6

Cannon

7

8
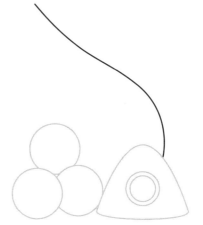

9
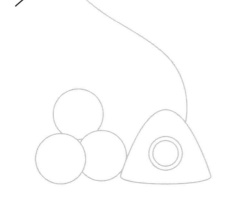

10
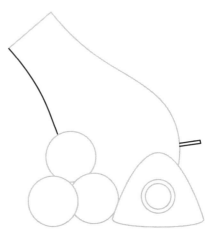

11
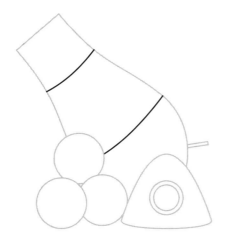

12
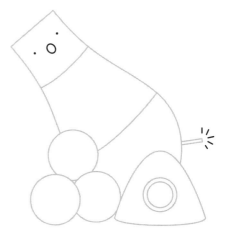

Pirates | 61

Pirate Hat

1

2

3

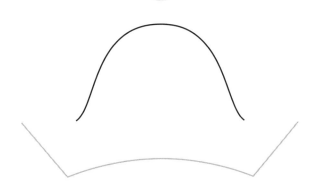

4

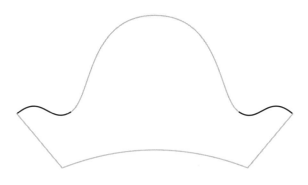

5

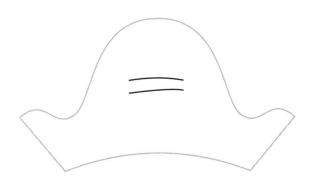

6

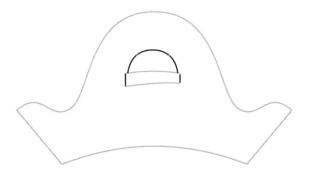

Pirate Hat

7
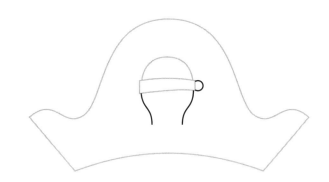

8
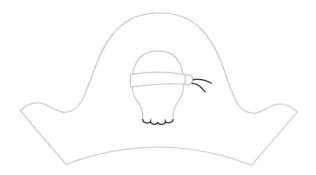

9
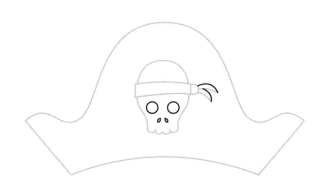

10

11
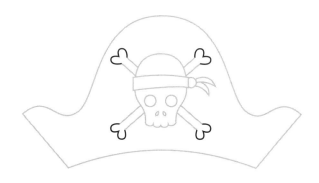

# Ship's Wheel

1

2

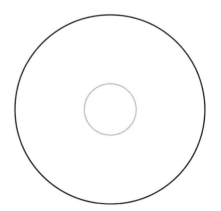

3

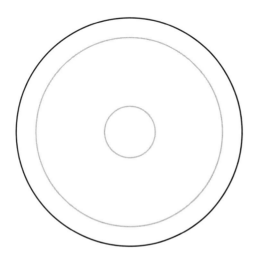

4

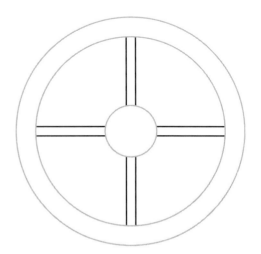

Ship's Wheel

5

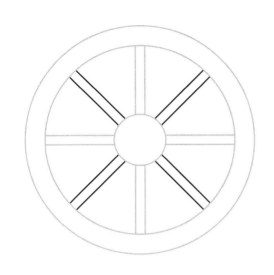

6

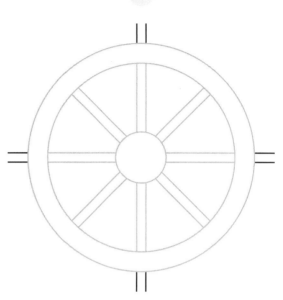

7

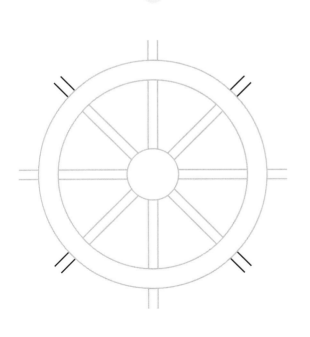

8

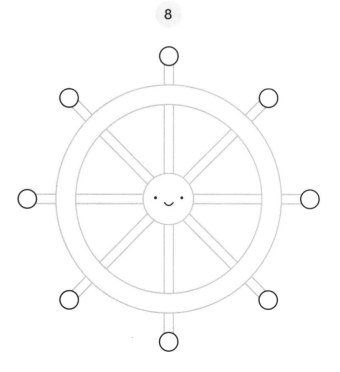

Pirates | 65

Anchor

1

2

3

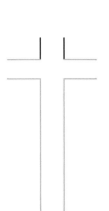

4

66 | Pirates

Anchor

5

6

7

8

Pirates | 67

# Pirate Boots

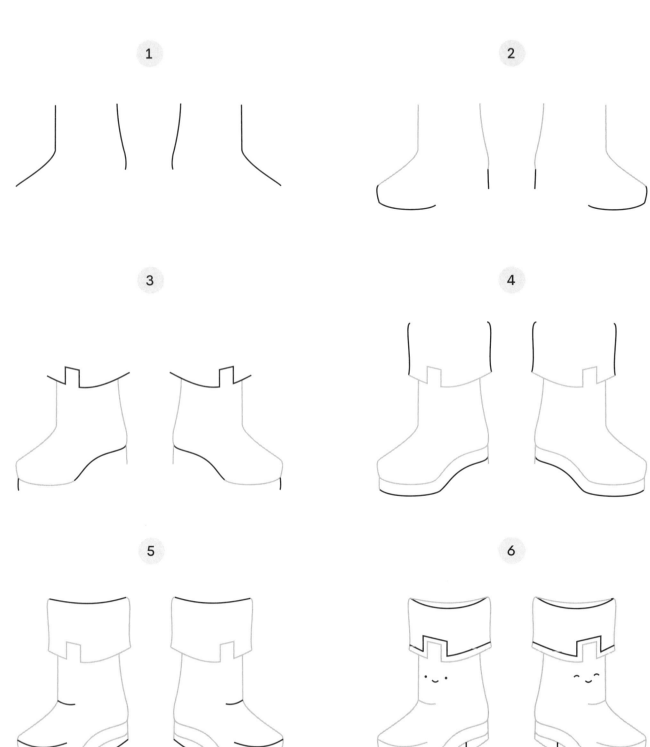

Bomb

1
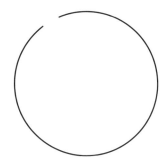

2

3

4

Pirates | 69

Parrot

1

2

3

4

5

6

Parrot

7

8

9

10

11

12
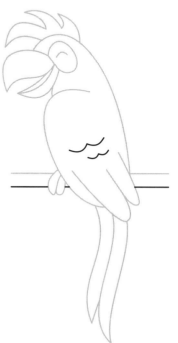

Pirates

Sports | 73

Basketball

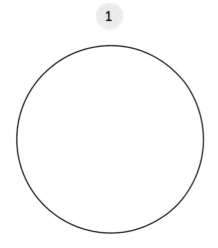
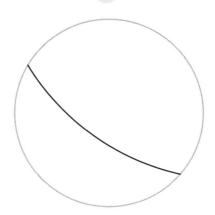
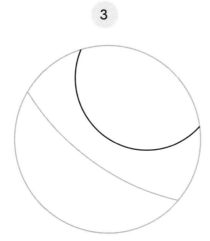
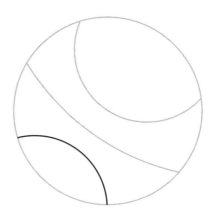
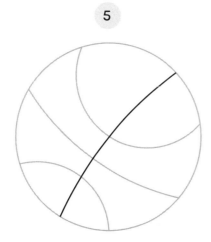
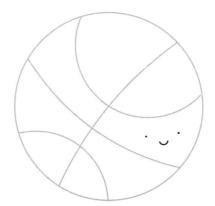

Baseball

1
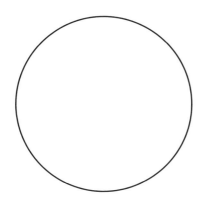

2
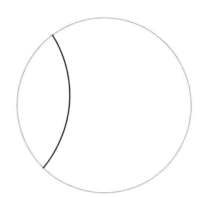

3
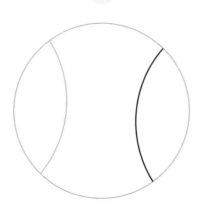

4
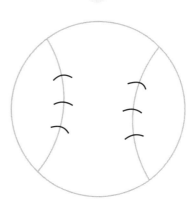

5
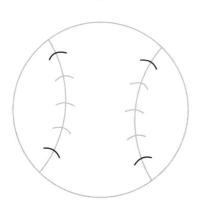

6
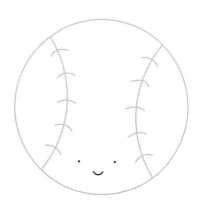

Sports | 75

Tennis Ball

1

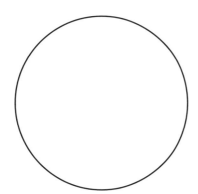

2

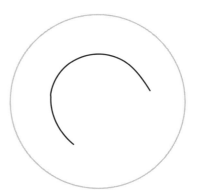

3

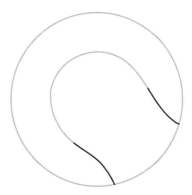

4

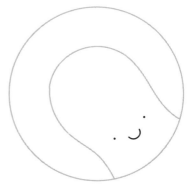

Football

1

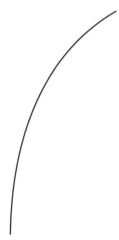

2 3

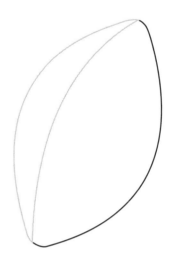

4

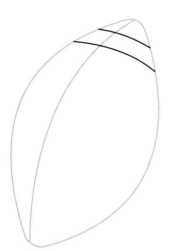

5

6

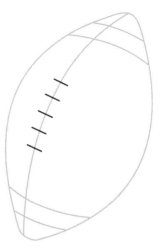

Sports | 77

Soccer Ball

1
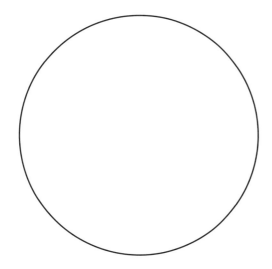

2
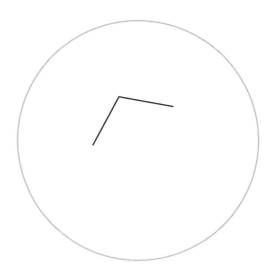

3
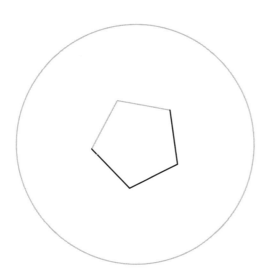

4
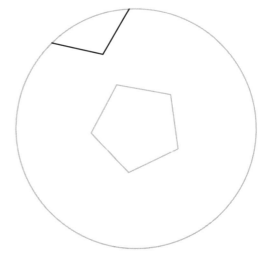

Soccer Ball

5

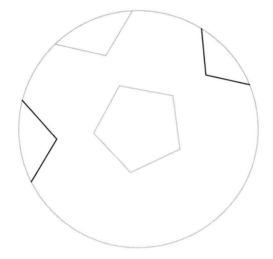

6

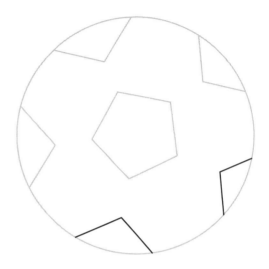

7

8

Volley Ball

1
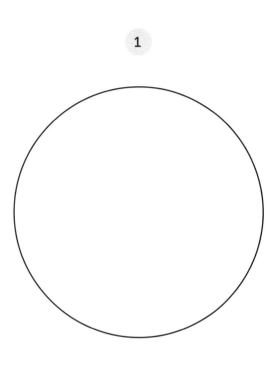

2

3
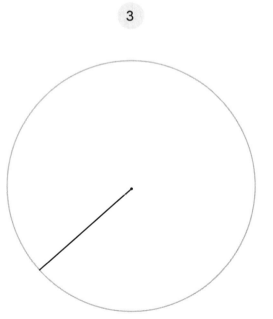

4
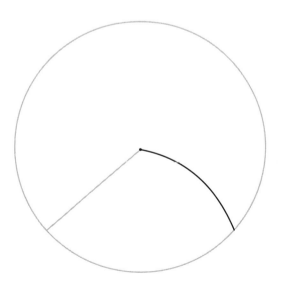

Volley Ball

5

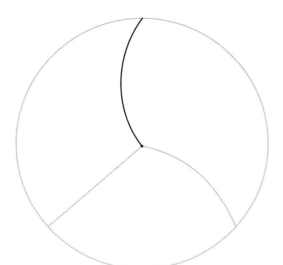

6

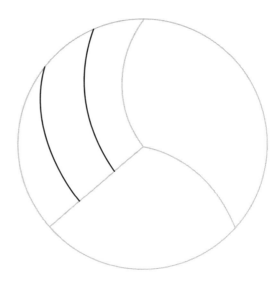

7

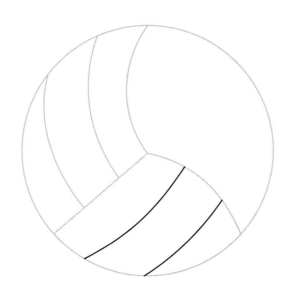

8

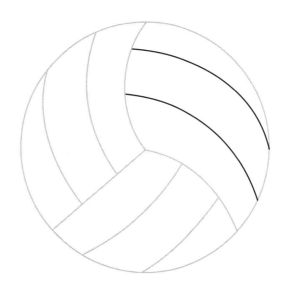

Sports | 81

Golf Ball

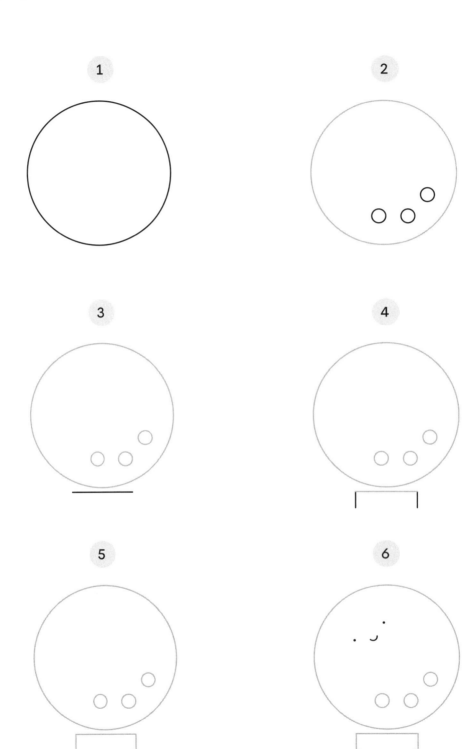

Hockey Stick and Puck

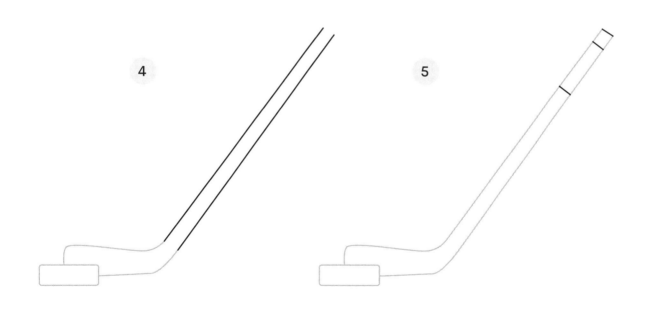

Sports | 83

Badminton Birdie

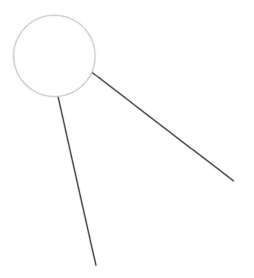

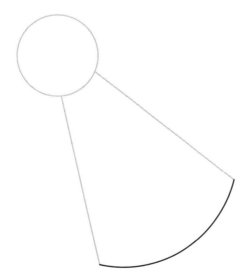

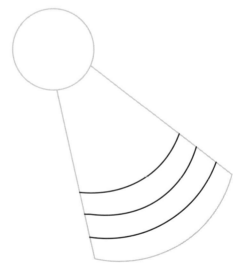

Badminton Birdie

5

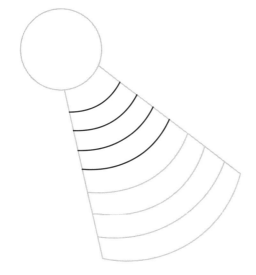

6

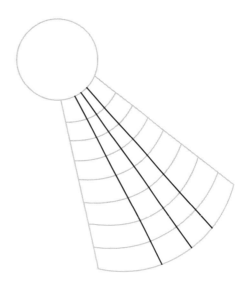

7

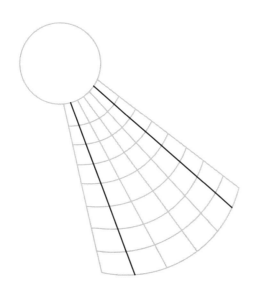

8

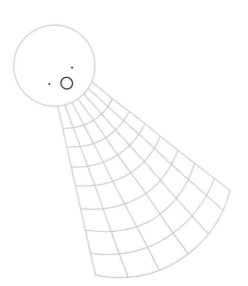

Sports | 85

Badminton Racket

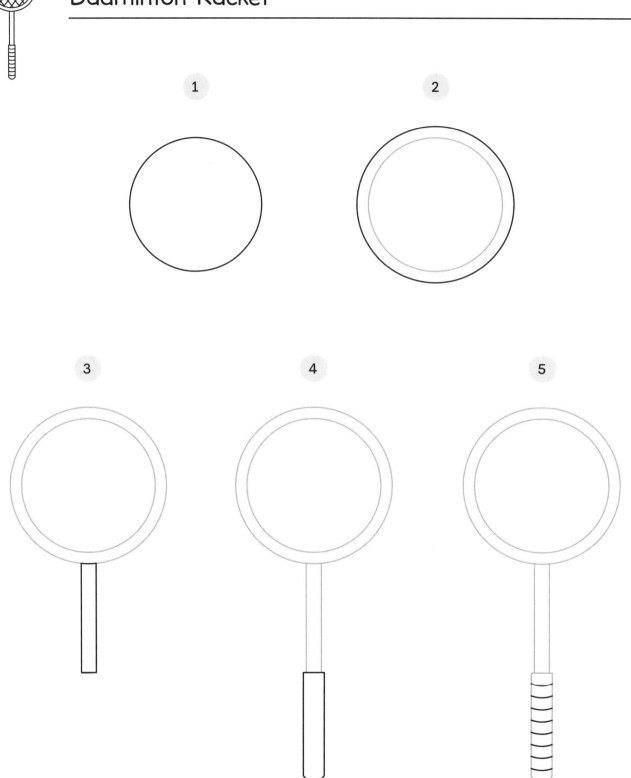

Badminton Racket

6
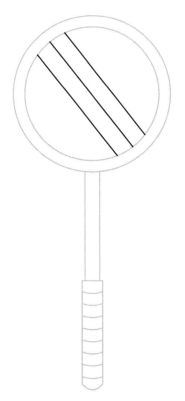

7

8
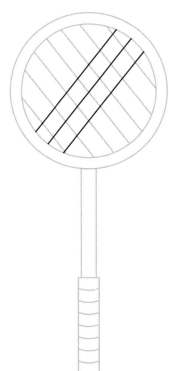

9
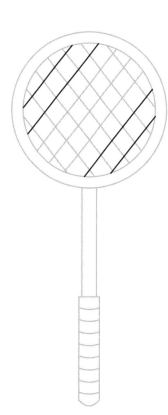

Tennis Racket

1
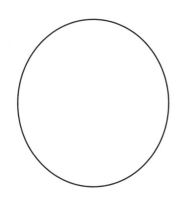

2
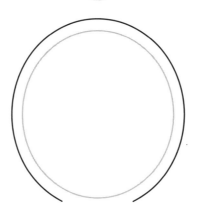

3
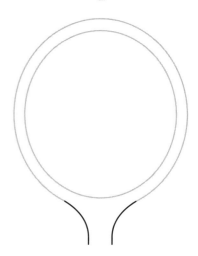

4

5
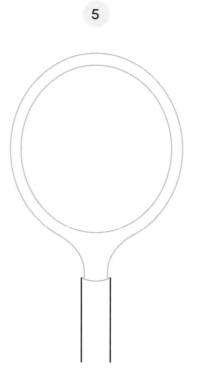

6
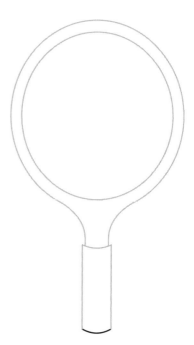

Sports

Tennis Racket

7

8

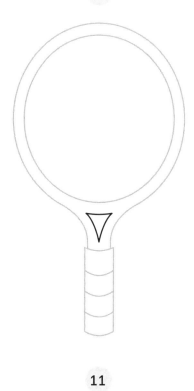

9

10

11

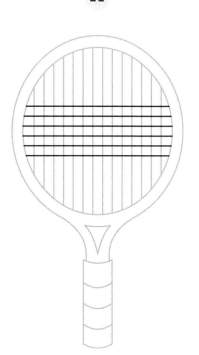

12

Sports | 89

Boxing Gloves

1

2

3

4

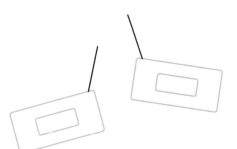

Boxing Gloves

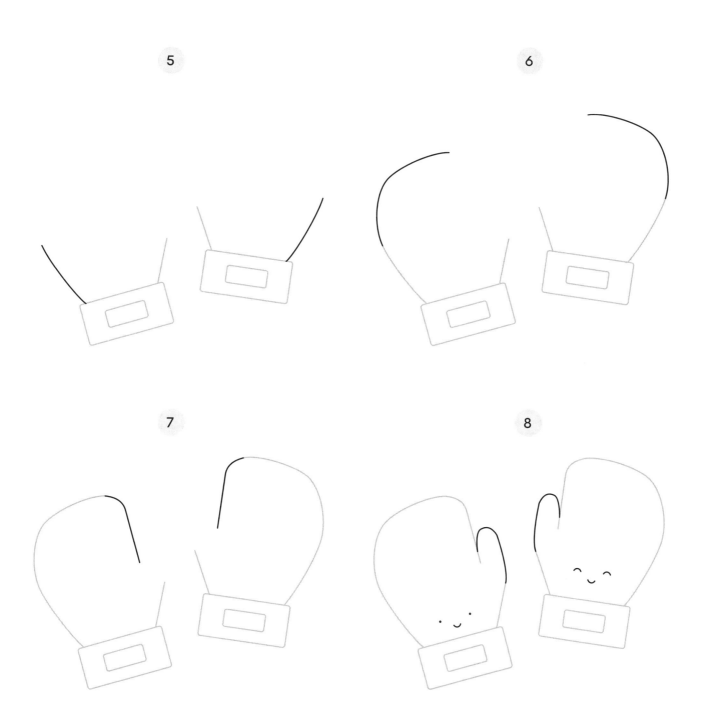

Megaphone

1

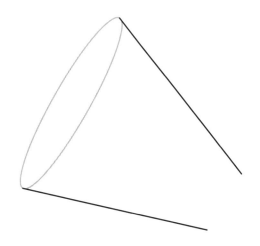

2

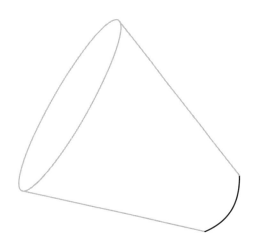

3

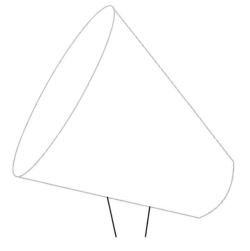

4

Megaphone

5

6

7

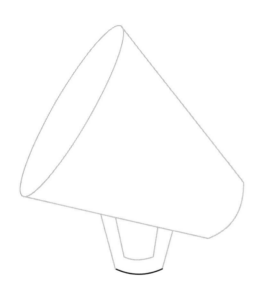

8

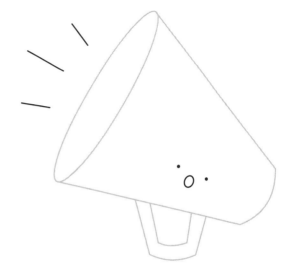

Stopwatch

1
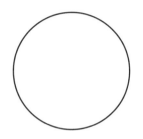

2
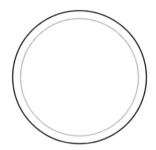

3

4
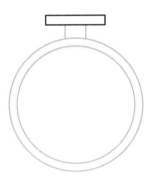

5

6
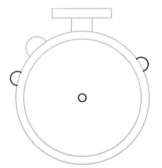

94 | Sports

Stopwatch

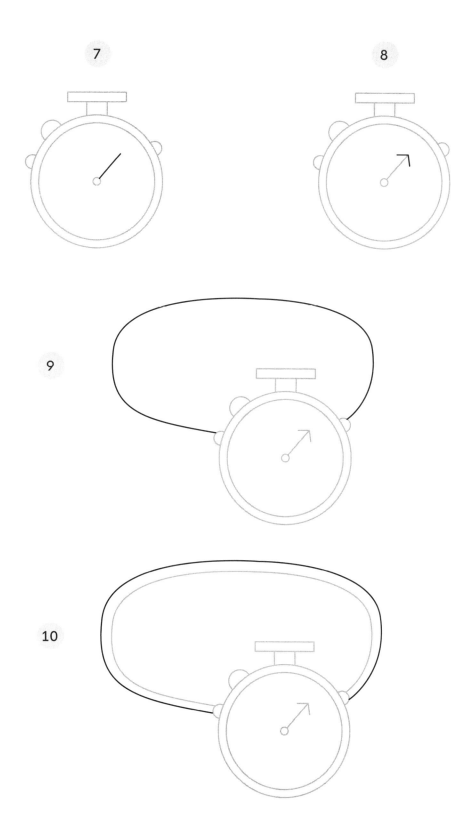

Sports | 95

Baseball Glove

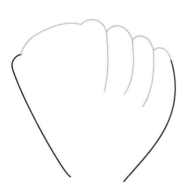

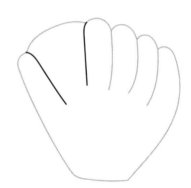

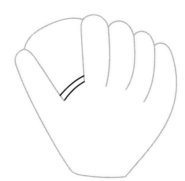

Baseball Glove

9

10

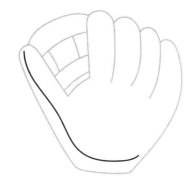

11

12

13

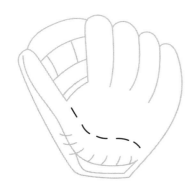

14

# Dumbbell

1
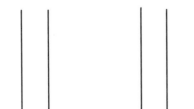

2

3

4
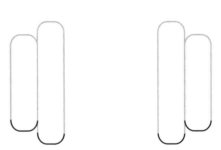

5
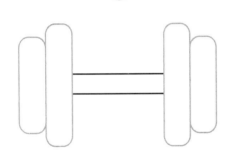

6
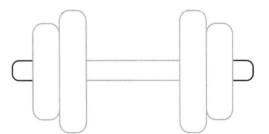

Baseball Bat

1

2
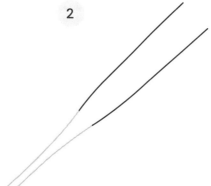

3

4
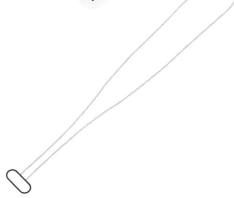

Pointe Shoes

1

2

3

4

5

6

7

8

9

100 | Sports

Pointe Shoes

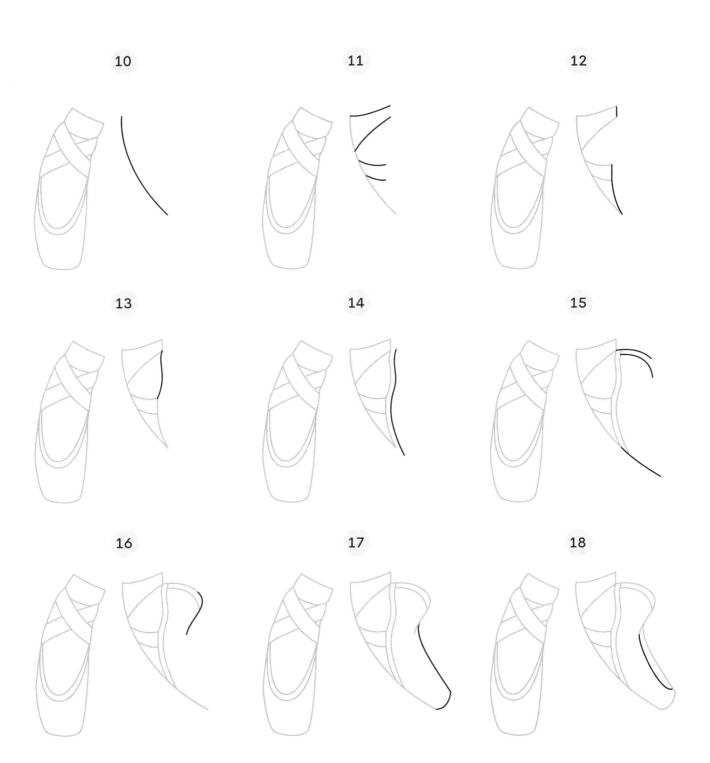

Sports | 101

# Snowboard

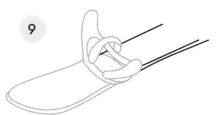

Sports

Snowboard

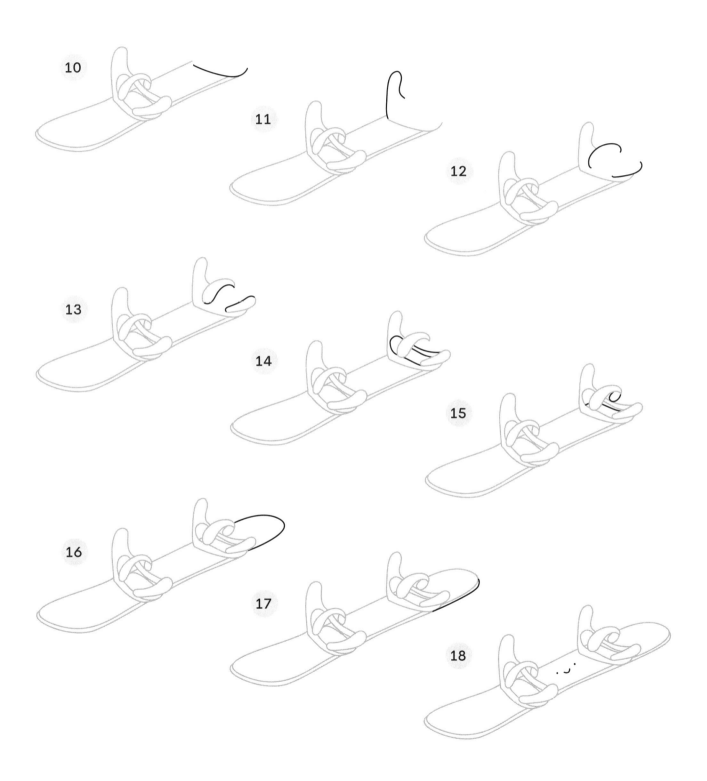

Downhill Skis

1

2

3

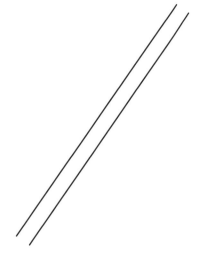

4

5

6

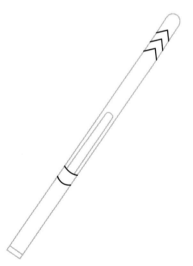

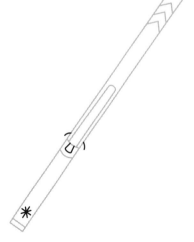

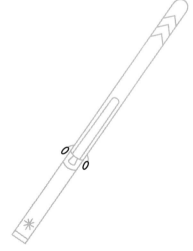

Downhill Skis

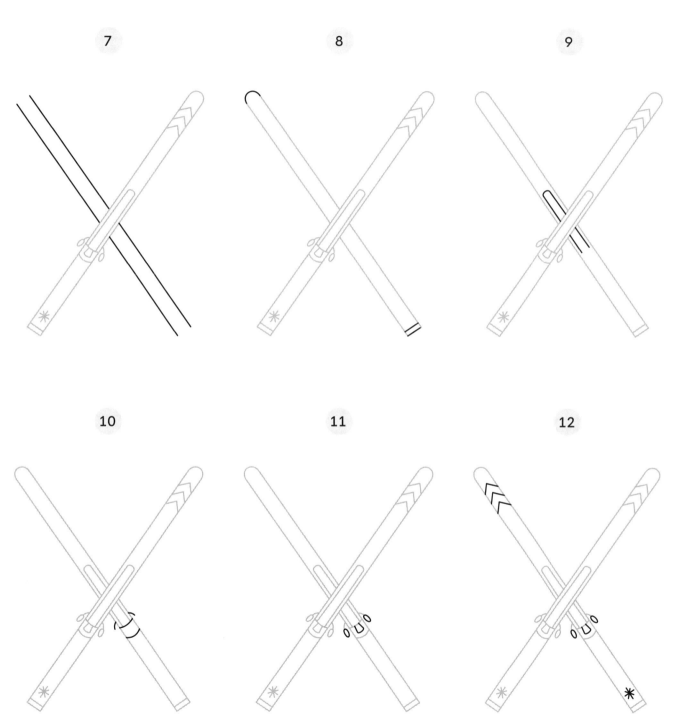

Trophy

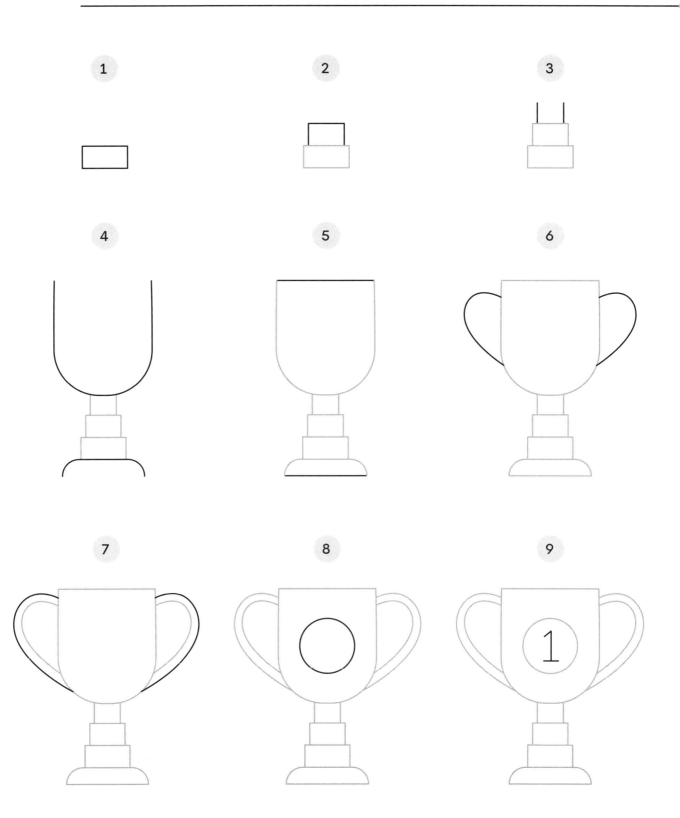

# Trumpet

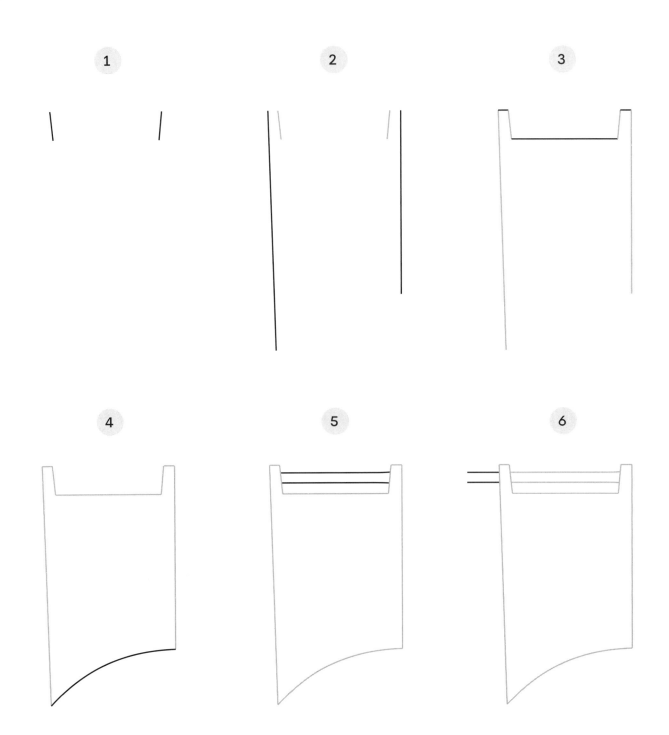

108 | Medieval Times

Trumpet

7

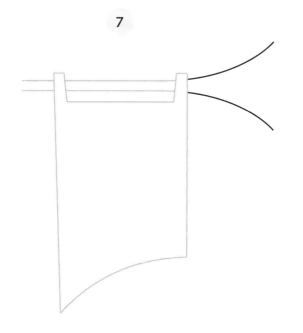

8

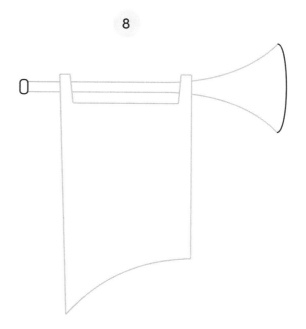

9

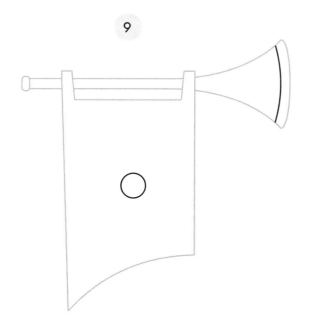

10

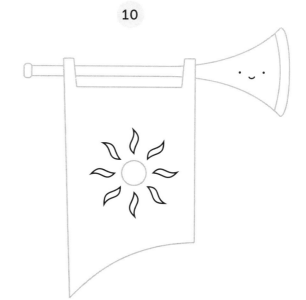

Medieval Times | 109

Swords

1

2

3
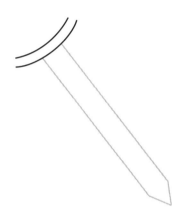

4
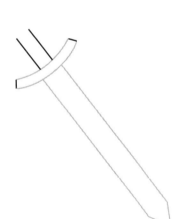

5
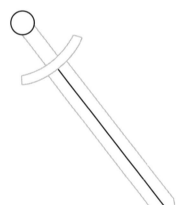

6
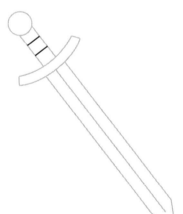

110 | Medieval Times

Swords

7

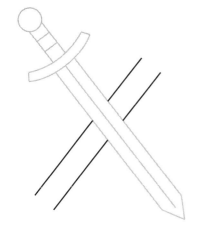

8

9

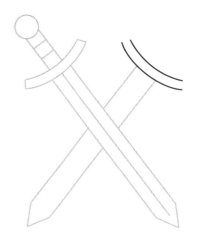

10

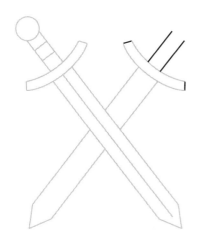

11

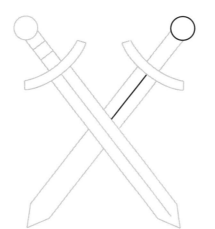

12

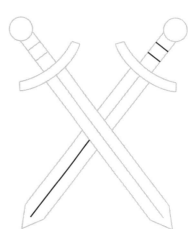

Medieval Times | 111

Shield

Medieval Times

Chalice

1

2

3

4
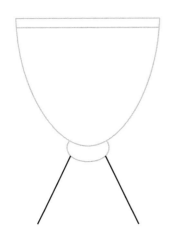

5
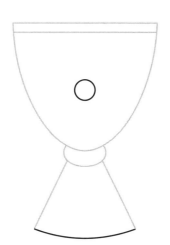

6
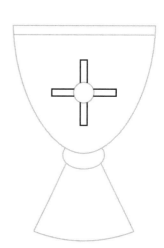

Medieval Times | 113

Axe

1.
2.
3.
4.
5.
6.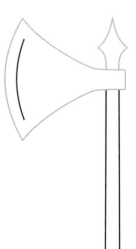

114 | Medieval Times

Axe

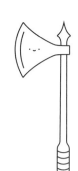

7
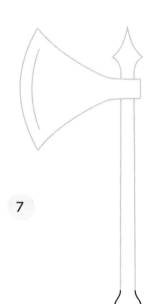

8
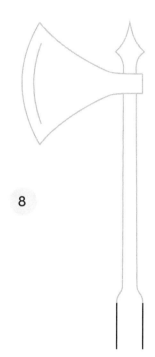

9
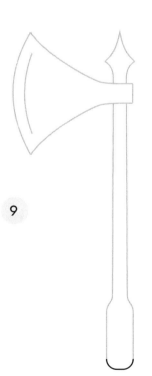

10
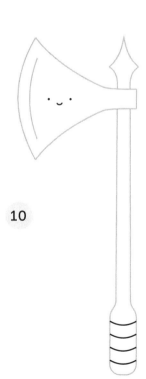

Medieval Times | 115

 # Mace

1

2

3

4

5
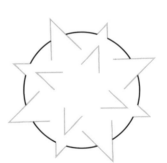

116 | Medieval Times

Mace

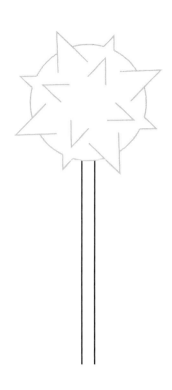

6

7

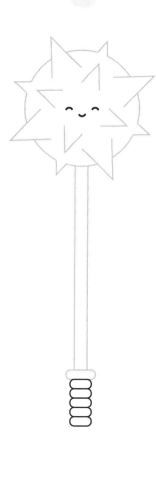

8

Medieval Times | 117

Tower

1

2

3

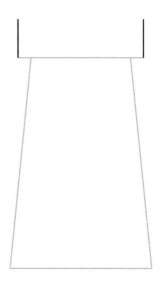

4

5

6

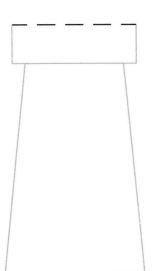

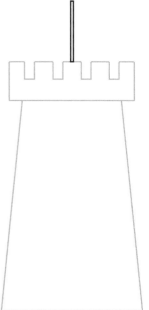

118 | Medieval Times

Tower

7

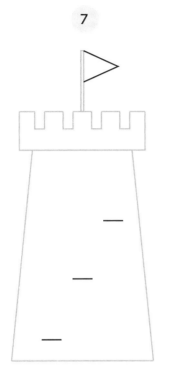

8

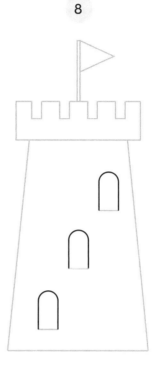

9

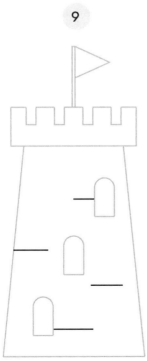

10

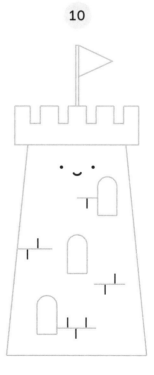

Medieval Times | 119

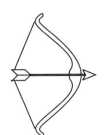

Bow and Arrow

1

2

3

4

5

6

Medieval Times

Bow and Arrow

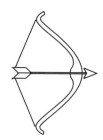

7
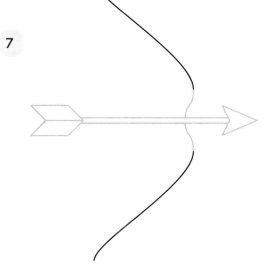

8
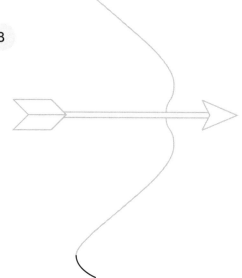

9
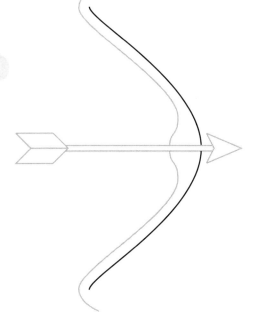

10
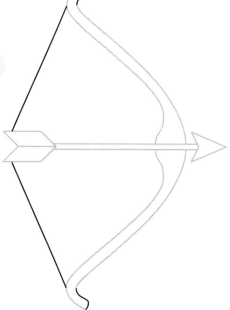

Medieval Times | 121

Helmet

1

2

3

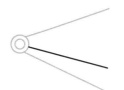

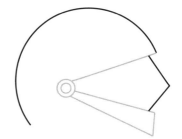

4

5

6

7

8

9

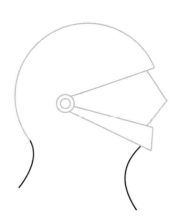

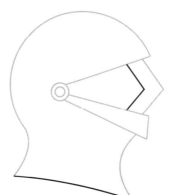

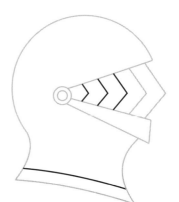

122 | Medieval Times

Helmet

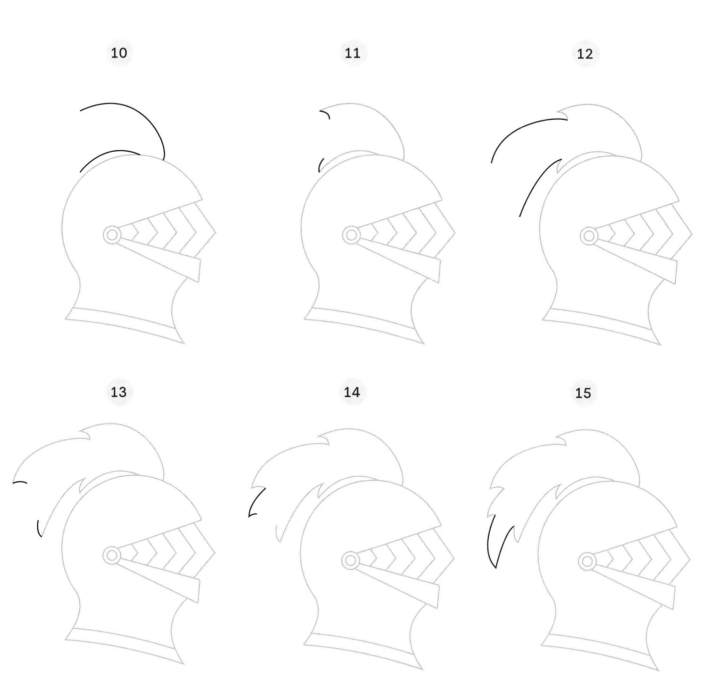

Medieval Times | 123

Quill and Ink

1
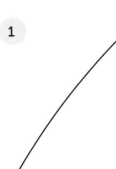

2
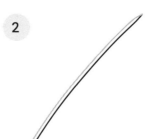

3
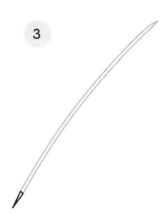

4
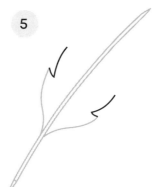

5

6
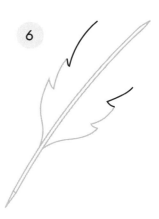

7

8
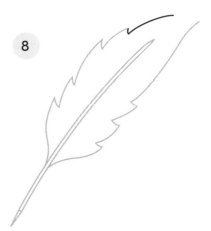

Quill and Ink

9

10

11

12

Medieval Times | 125

Jester's Hat

1

2

3

4

5
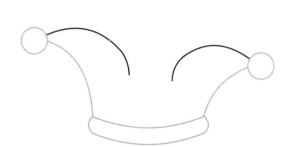

6
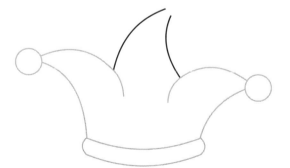

Jester's Hat

7

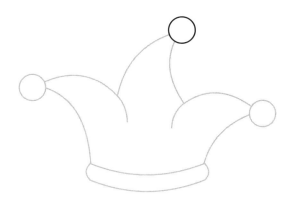

8

9

10

Medieval Times | 127

Catapult

1

2

3

4

5

6

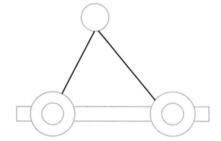

7

8

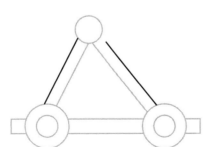 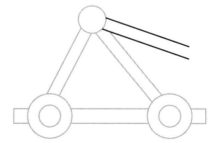

Catapult

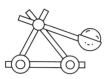

9

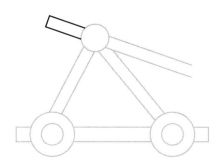

10

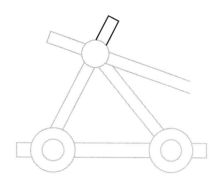

11

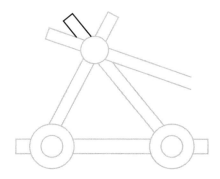

12

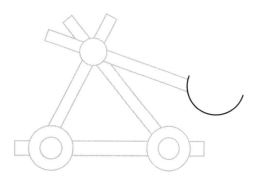

13

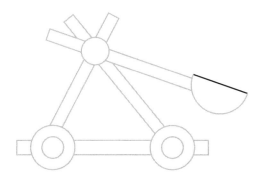

14

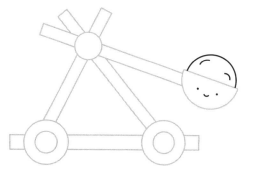

Medieval Times | 129

Visor

1
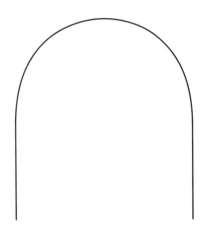

2
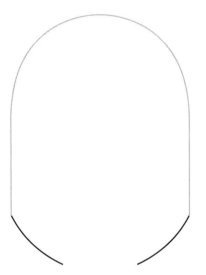

3
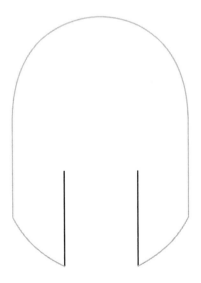

4
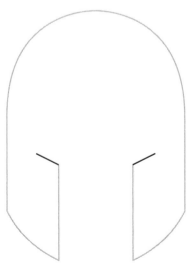

Visor

5
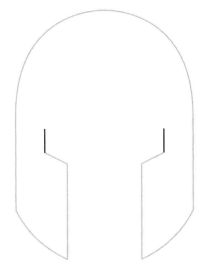

6
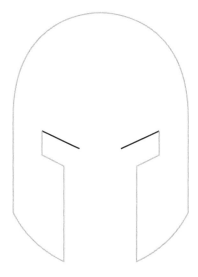

7
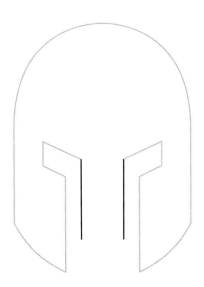

8
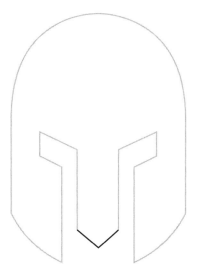

Medieval Times

 # Double Headed Battle Axe

1

2

3

4
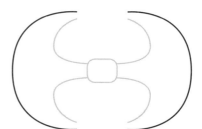

Double Headed Battle Axe

5

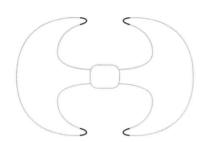

6

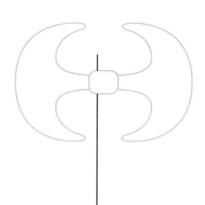

7

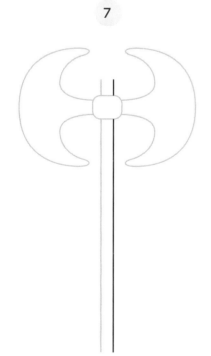

8

Medieval Times | 133

Battle Horse

1
2
3
4
5
6
7
8
9
10
11
12

134 | Medieval Times

Battle Horse

13

14

15

16

17

18

19

Medieval Times | 135

Knight

1
2
3

4
5
6

7
8
9

136 | Medieval Times

Knight

10

11

12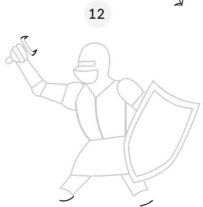

13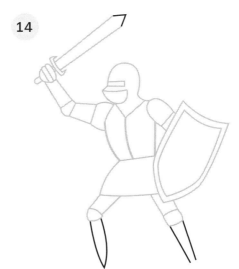

14

15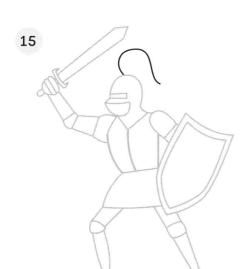

16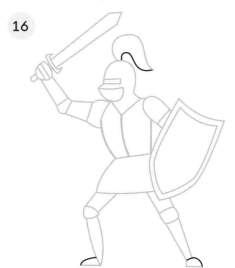

Medieval Times | 137

Crown

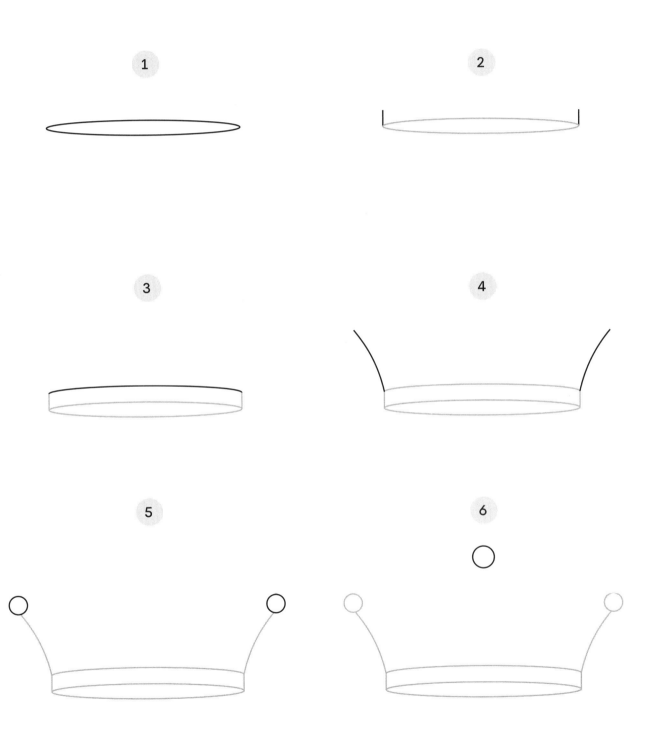

Crown

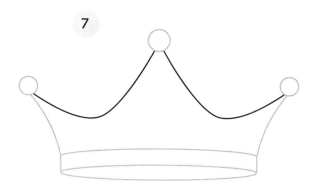

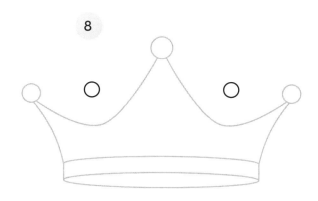

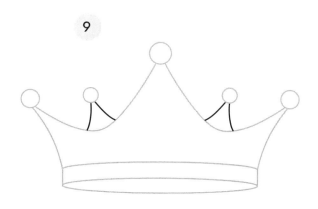

Dragon

1

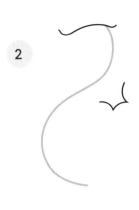
2

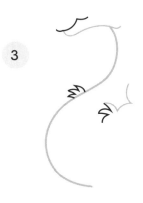
3

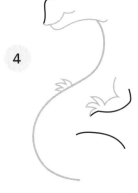
4

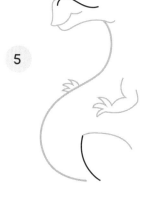
5

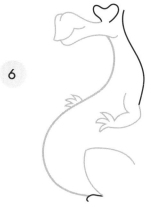
6

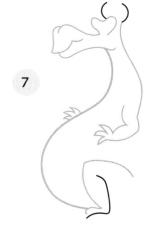
7

8

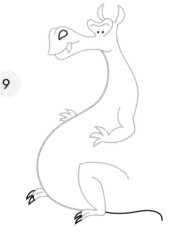
9

140 | Medieval Times

Dragon

10
11
12
13
14
15
16

Medieval Times | 141

Cauldron

1

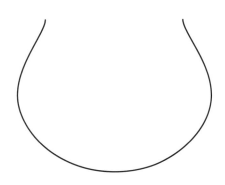

2

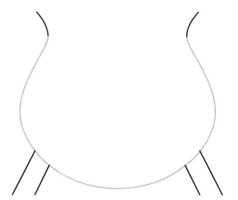

3

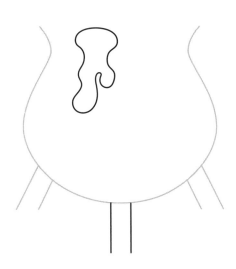

4

142 | Medieval Times

Cauldron

5

6

7

8

Medieval Times | 143

# Magic Potion

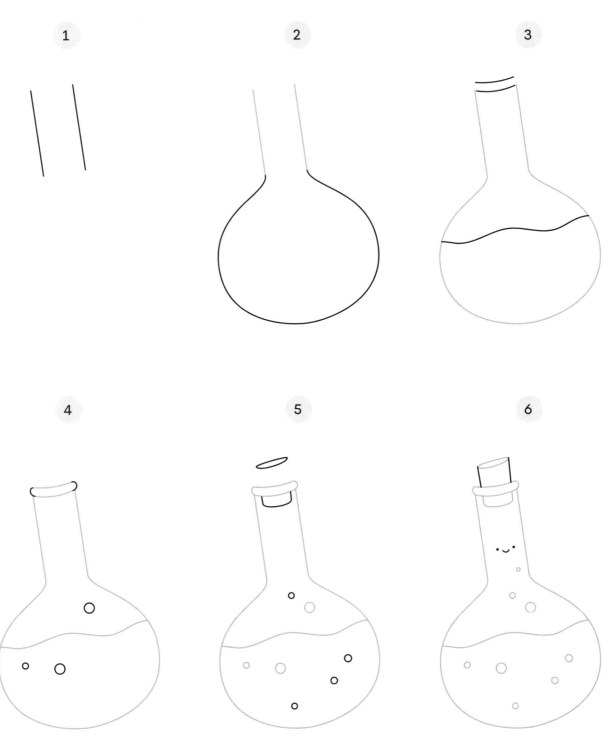

 # Propeller Plane

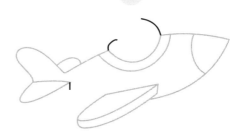

Things That Go

Propeller Plane

9
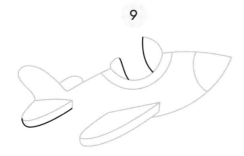

10
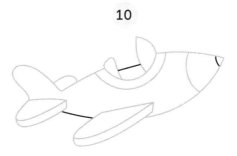

11
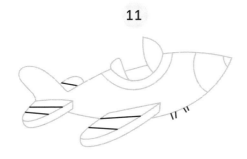

12
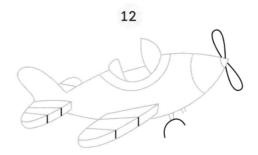

13
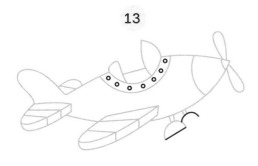

14
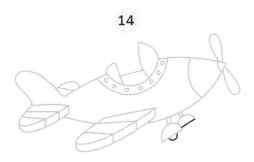

15
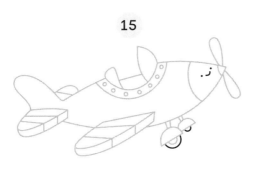

16
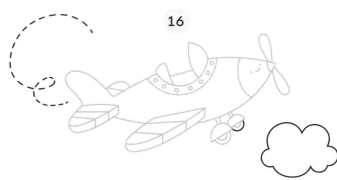

Things That Go | 147

 # Helicopter

1

2
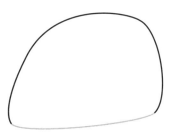

3
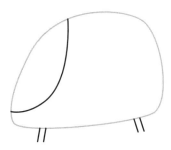

4

5
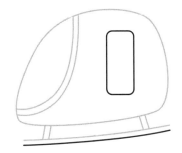

6
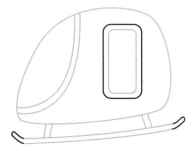

Helicopter

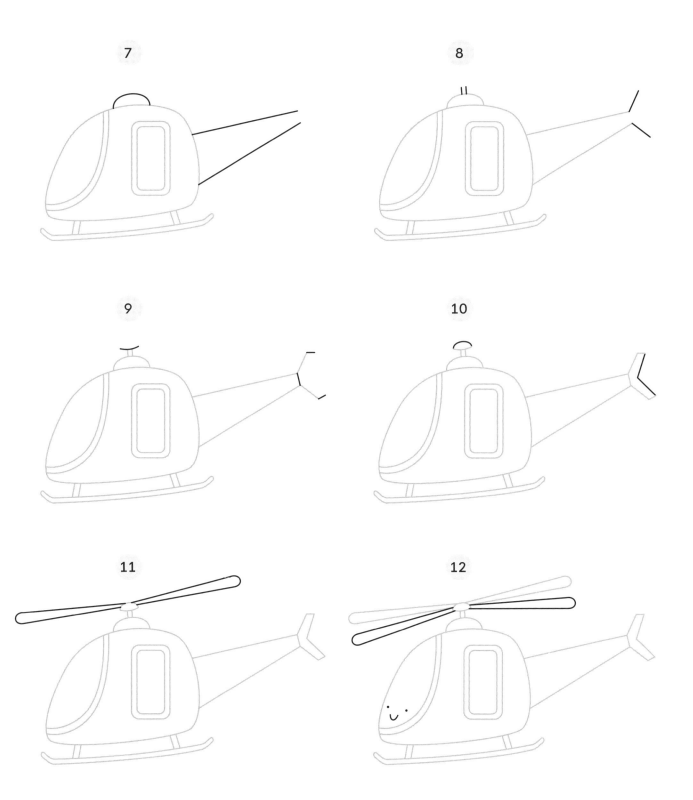

Things That Go | 149

# Jet

1

2

3

4

5

6
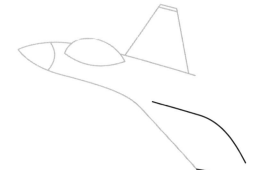

Things That Go

Jet

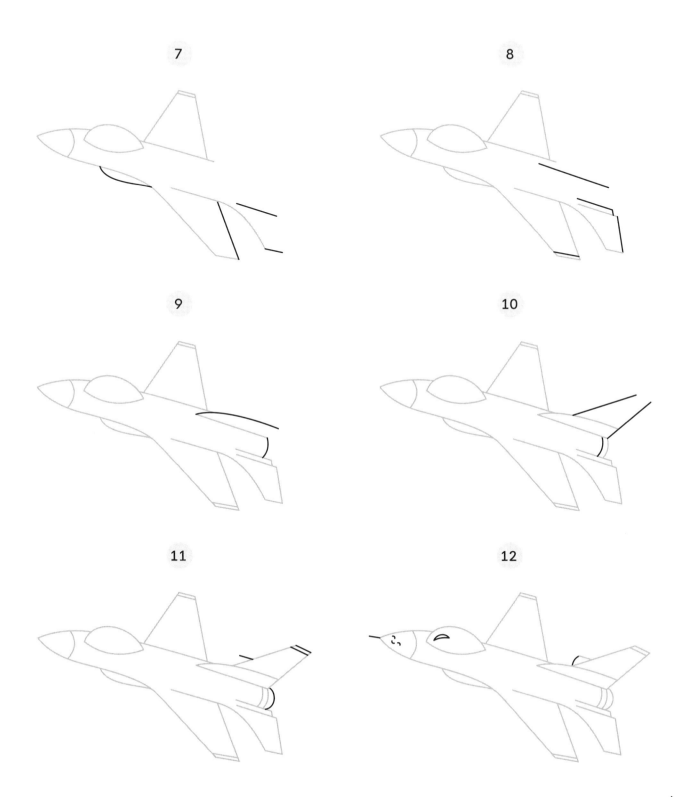

Things That Go

Hot Air Balloon

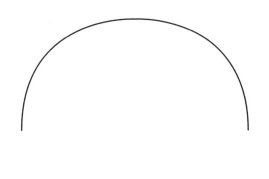

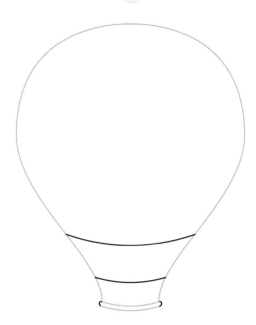

Hot Air Balloon

5

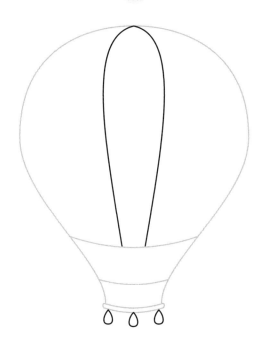

6

7

8

Things That Go | 153

Sail Boat

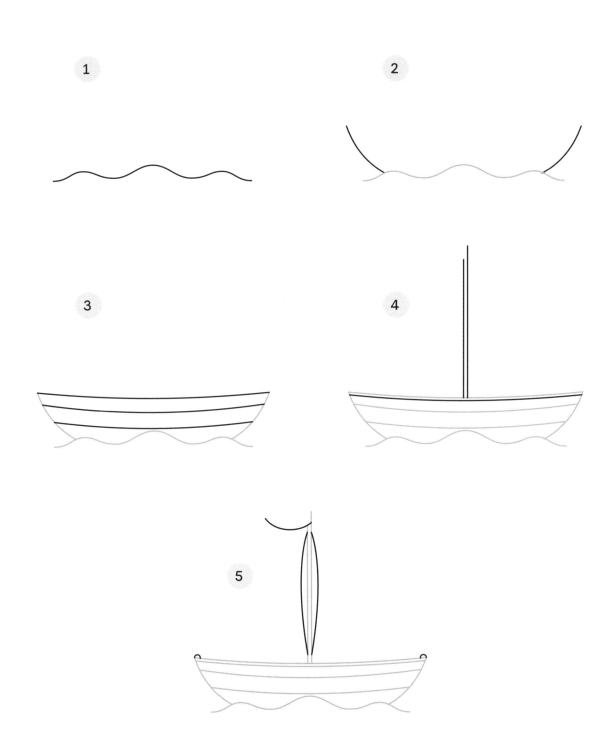

Sail Boat

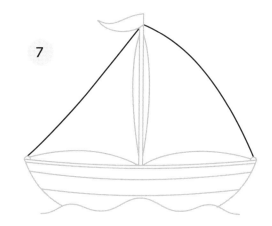
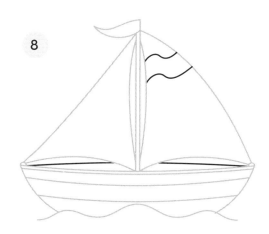
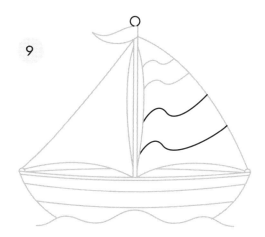
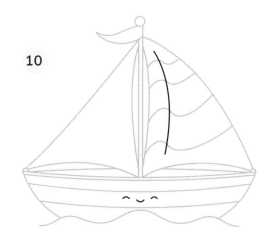

Things That Go

Speed Boat

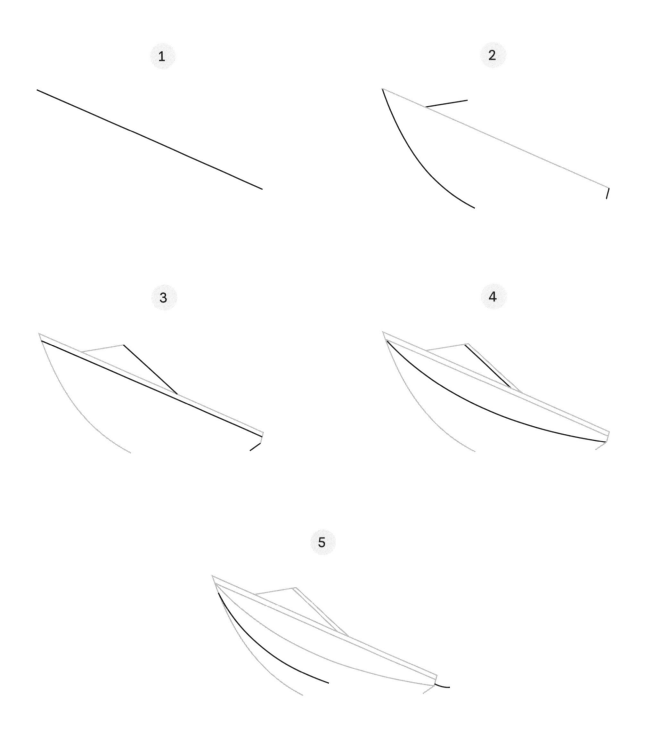

Speed Boat

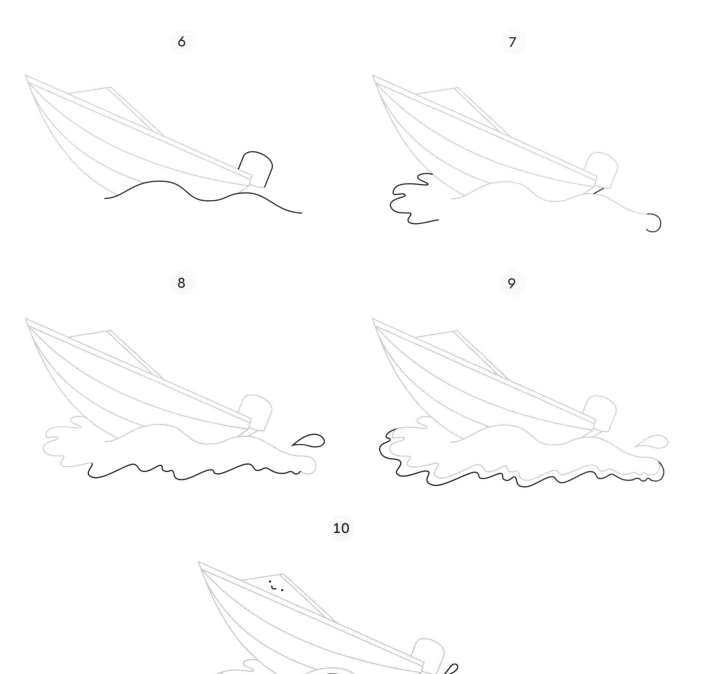

Things That Go | 157

 # Bicycle

1

2

3

4

5

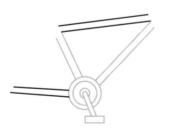

6

Bicycle

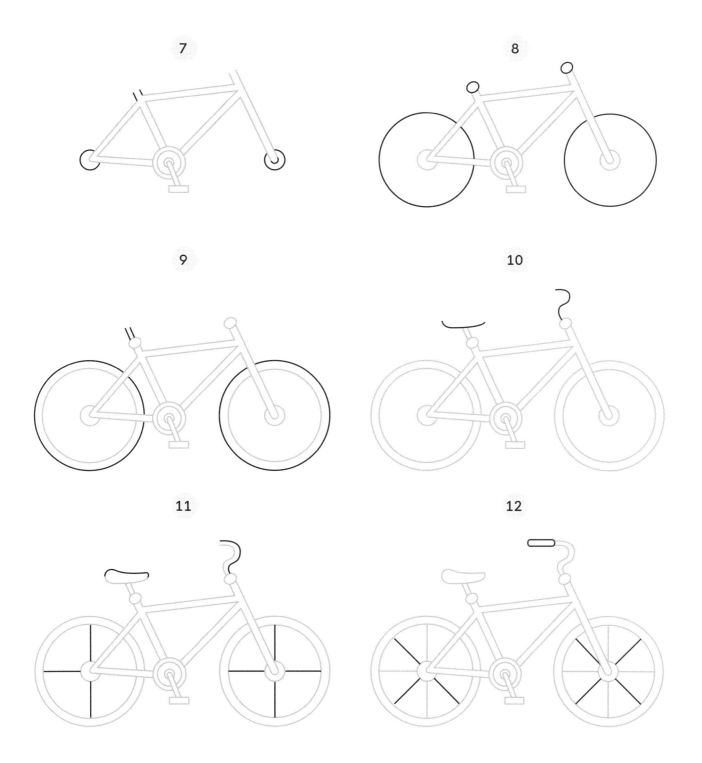

Things That Go

Motor Scooter

1

2

3
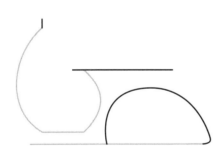

4
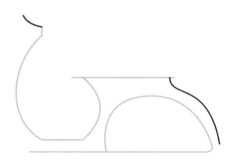

5
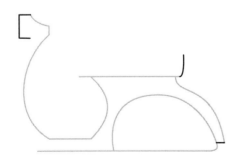

6
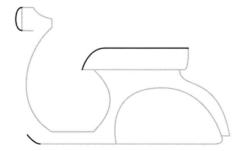

160 | Things That Go

Motor Scooter

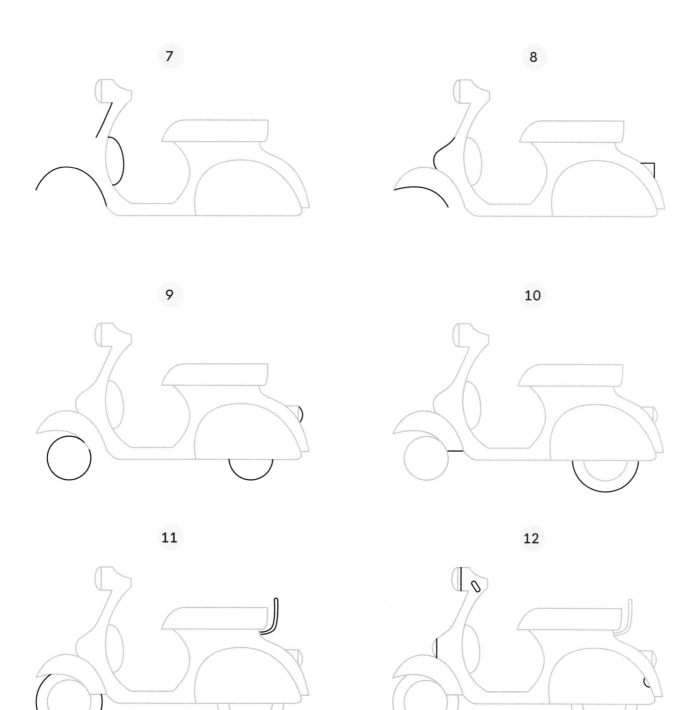

Things That Go

Motorcycle

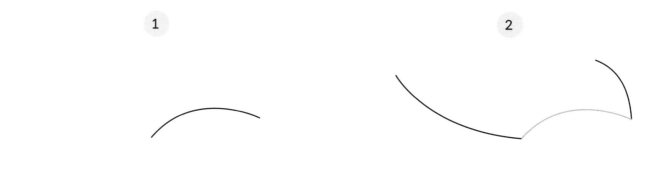

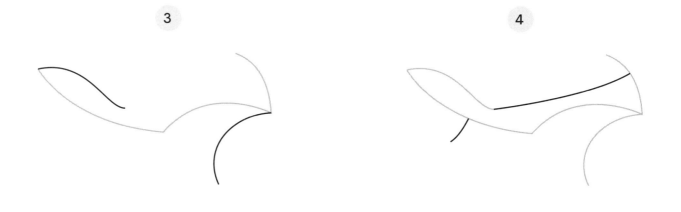

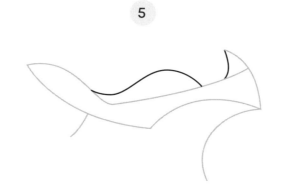

Motorcycle

6

7
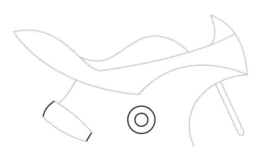

8
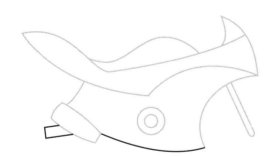

9
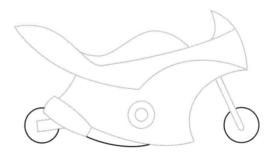

10

Things That Go

 Race Car

1

2

3

4

Race Car

5
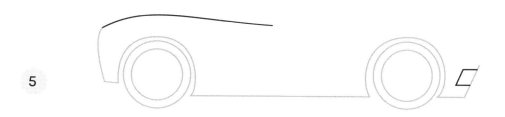

6
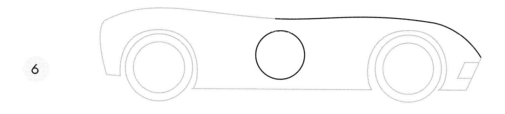

7
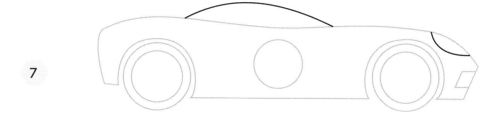

8
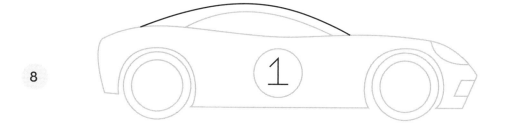

# Family Van

Family Van

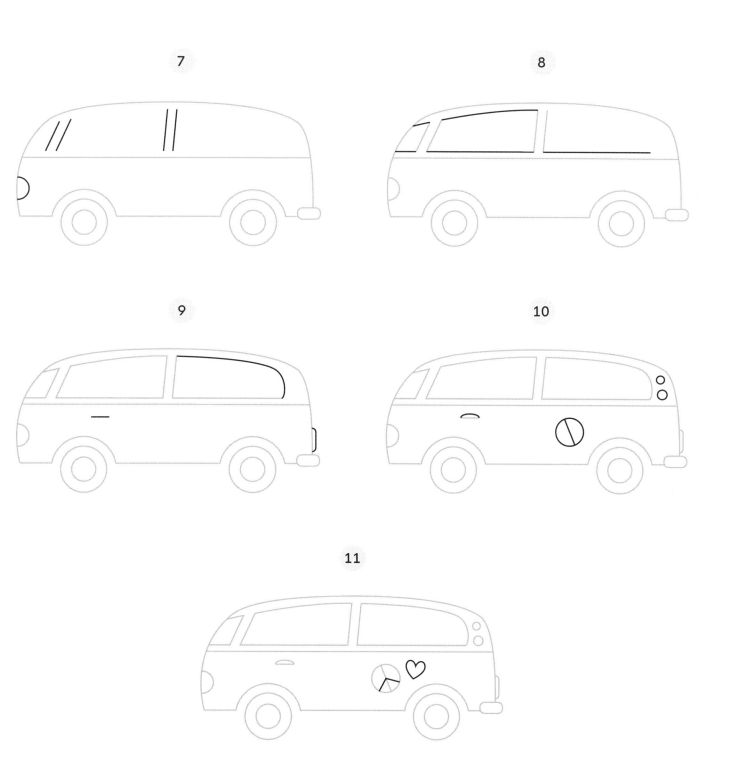

Things That Go | 167

# School Bus

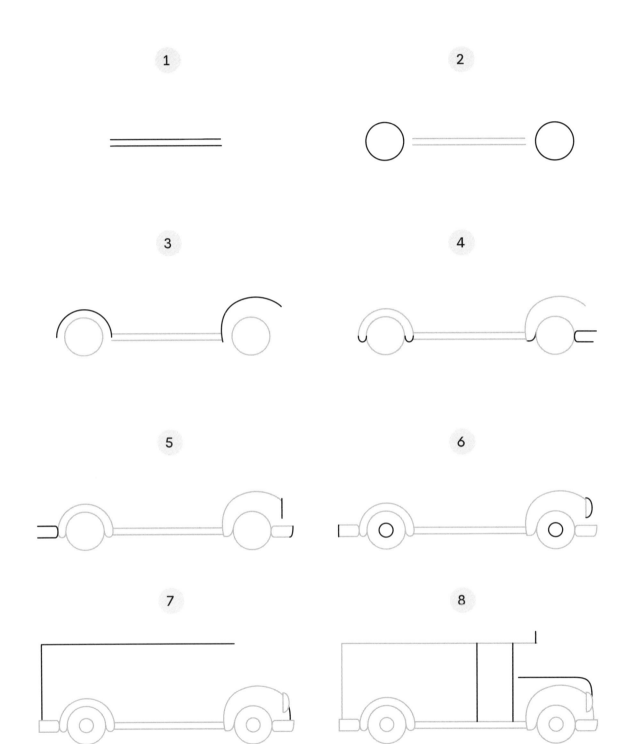

168 | Things That Go

School Bus

 City Bus

1

2

3

4

City Bus

5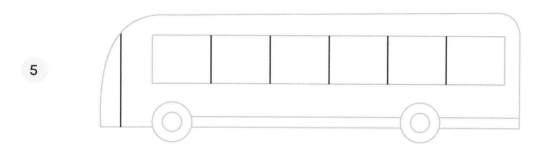

6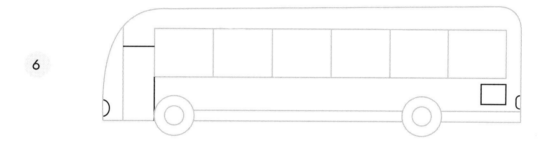

7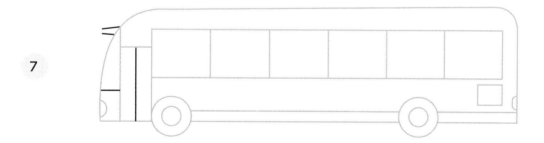

8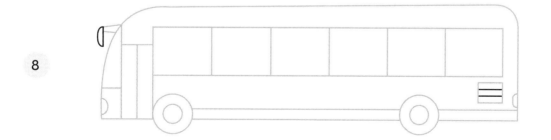

 # Dump Truck

1

2

3

4

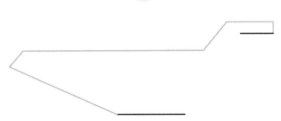

5

6

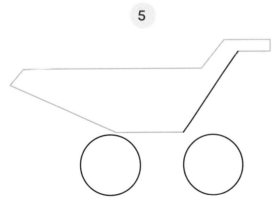

Dump Truck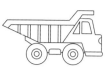

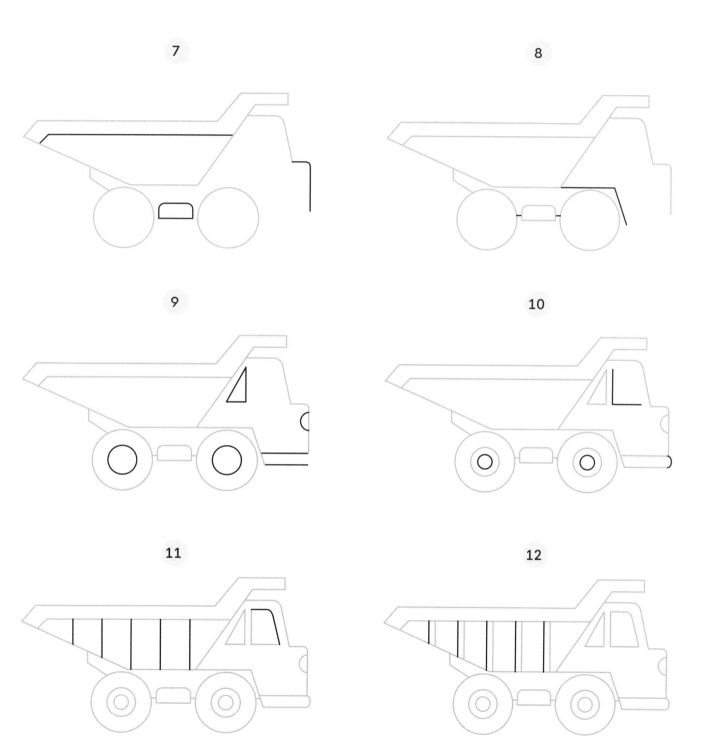

# Excavator

1
2
3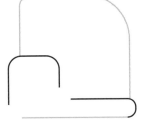
4
5
6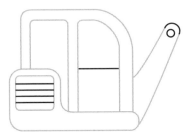
7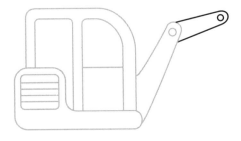
8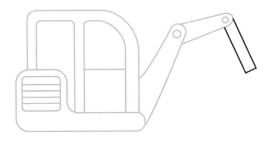

Things That Go

Excavator

9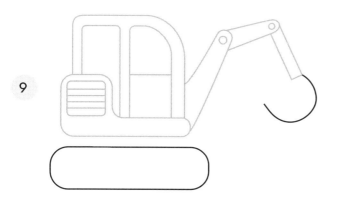

10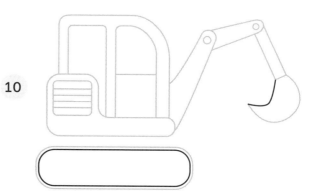

11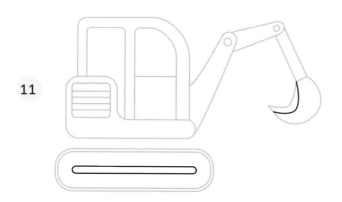

12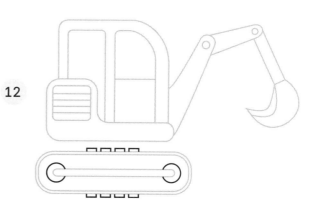

13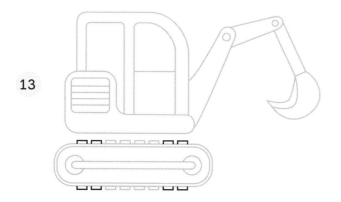

14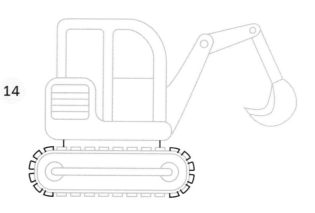

Things That Go | 175

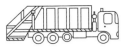 # Garbage Truck

1

2

3
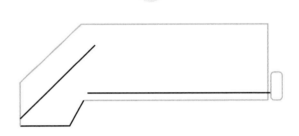

4

5
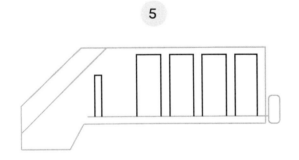

6
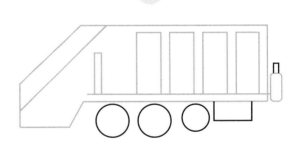

7
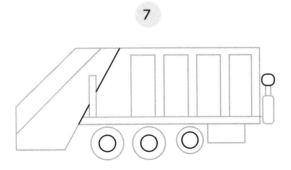

8
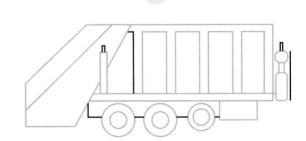

Garbage Truck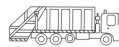

9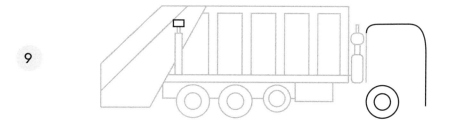

10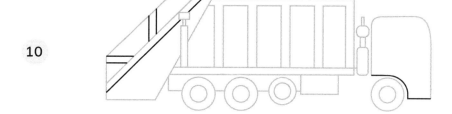

11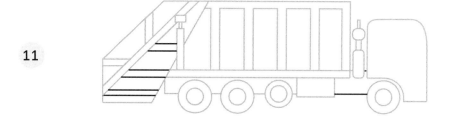

12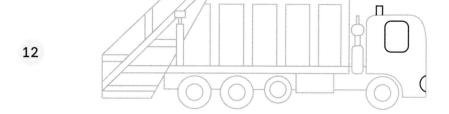

13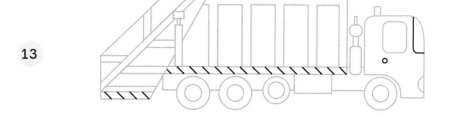

Things That Go | 177

 # Fire Engine

Fire Engine

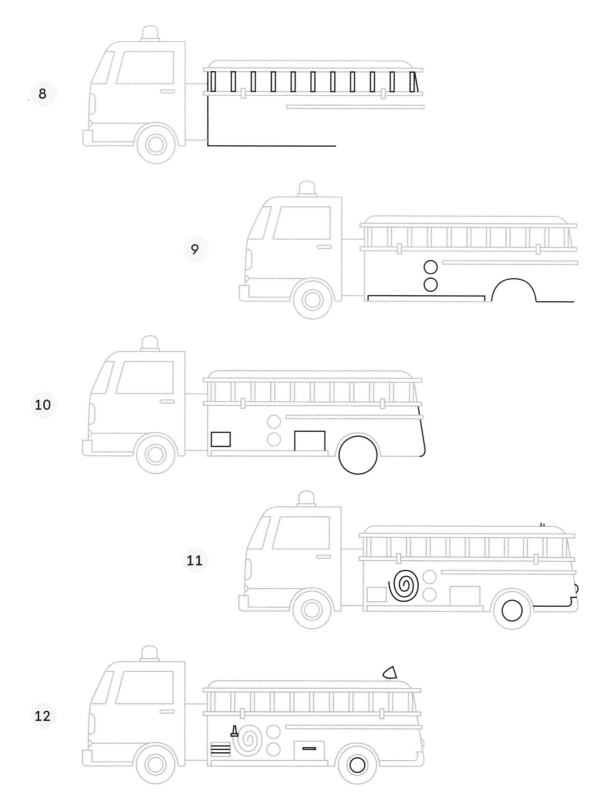

Things That Go | 179

Police Car

1

2

3

4

5

6

180 | Things That Go

Police Car

7

8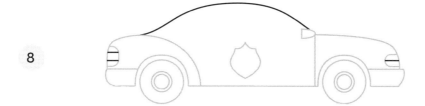

9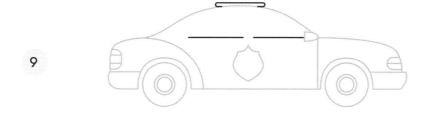

10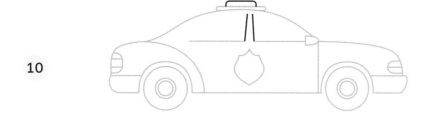

11

Things That Go

 # Ambulance

1

2

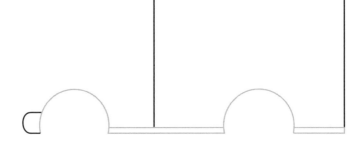
3

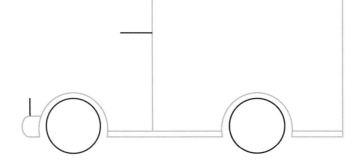
4

Ambulance

5

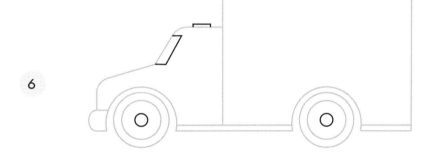

6

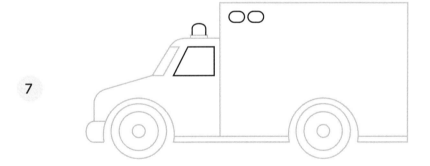

7

8

Things That Go | 183

Check out the original *How to Draw Book for Kids* for even more drawing fun! Available for purchase on Amazon.

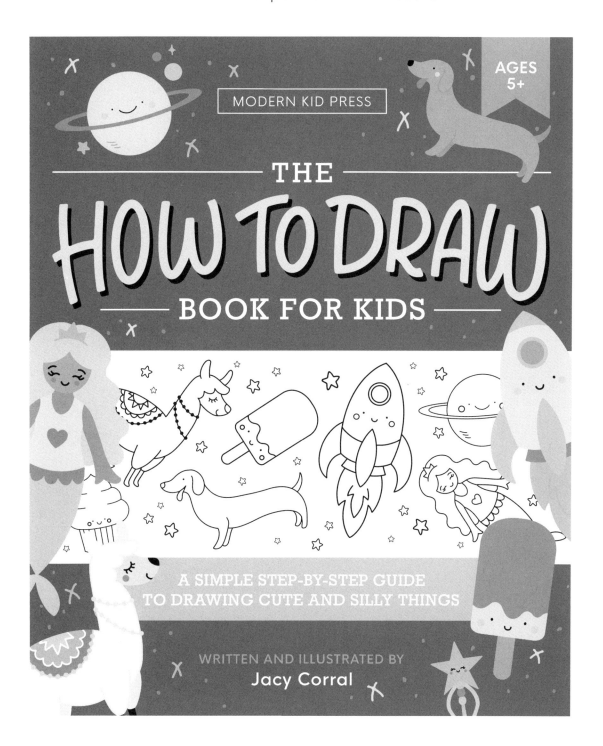